QUEER AND TRANS PEOPLE OF COLOUR IN THE UK

This book explores the meanings of Queer and Trans People of Colour (QTPOC) activist groups in the UK, considering the tensions around inclusion and belonging across lesbian, gay, bisexual, trans, and queer (LGBTQ) and of colour communities and wider British society.

Davis draws de-/anti-/post-colonial, Black feminist, and queer theory into critical psychology to publish the first book of its kind in the UK, developing an intersectional understanding of QTPOC subjectivities and identities. The book examines questions of belonging; racial melancholia; decolonising gender and sexualities; and the joys, erotics, and the difficulties of building and finding QTPOC community that can hold and celebrate our intersectional richness.

Offering a radical and critical intervention into psychology, this volume will be of key interest to scholars in Gender Studies and Queer Studies, Psychology and Race, together with activists, community organisers, counsellors, and the third sector.

Stephanie Davis is a scholar-activist, a Black queer troublemaker, and a Senior Lecturer in Critical Psychology and Race at Nottingham Trent University. She has a specific interest in the intersections of race, gender, and sexuality; critical psychology; decolonial, queer, and Black feminist theory; critical pedagogies; and decolonising academia. She has previously worked in a community development and activist capacity on issues of sexual health with young people and Black and brown communities and on issues facing her local community such as police harassment and gender and sexual diversity. In 2013, she co-founded Rainbow Noir, a social support and organising space for QTPOC in Manchester. Stephanie has previously held Lectureships at the University of Brighton and the University of East London. She was also a Research Officer on the NIHR-funded

Queer Futures 2 project which explored how to improve mental health provision for LGBTQ youth in the UK. As an educator she is inspired by bell hooks' 'education as the practice of freedom' and strives to create learning environments with her students that encourage openness, dialogue, debate, and critical thinking. As a scholar-activist she is excited by the possibilities of working both within academia and beyond its boundaries.

Transforming LGBTQ Lives
Series Editors:
Katherine Johnson (RMIT University, Australia)
Kath Browne (University College Dublin, Ireland)

Transforming LGBTQ Lives hosts the best international scholarship on contemporary Lesbian, Gay, Bi, Trans and Queer (LGBTQ) issues. Innovative, interdisciplinary and intersectional, the series showcases theoretical and empirical research that fosters debate, pushes disciplinary boundaries and shapes activism. Extending feminist and queer scholarship through attention to a wide set of disciplinary influences (sociology, psychology, human geography, media and cultural studies, social policy, leisure studies, sports studies, political science) topics address the diversity of LGBTQ lives.

Recent titles in series:

The Everyday Lives of Gay Men
Autoethnographies of the Ordinary
Edited by Edgar Rodríguez-Dorans and Jason Holmes

Queer Roma
Lucie Fremlova

Queer Kinship on the Edge? Families of Choice in Poland
Joanna Mizielińska

Queer and Trans People of Colour in the UK
Possibilities for Intersectional Richness
Stephanie Davis

For more information about this series, please visit: www.Routledge.com/Transforming-LGBTQ-Lives/book-series/LGBTQLIVES

QUEER AND TRANS PEOPLE OF COLOUR IN THE UK

Possibilities for Intersectional Richness

Stephanie Davis

Routledge
Taylor & Francis Group

LONDON AND NEW YORK

Designed cover image: ANASTASIIA DMITRIEVA / Getty Images

First published 2023
by Routledge
4 Park Square, Milton Park, Abingdon, Oxon OX14 4RN

and by Routledge
605 Third Avenue, New York, NY 10158

Routledge is an imprint of the Taylor & Francis Group, an informa business

© 2023 Stephanie Davis

The right of Stephanie Davis to be identified as author of this work has been asserted in accordance with sections 77 and 78 of the Copyright, Designs and Patents Act 1988.

All rights reserved. No part of this book may be reprinted or reproduced or utilised in any form or by any electronic, mechanical, or other means, now known or hereafter invented, including photocopying and recording, or in any information storage or retrieval system, without permission in writing from the publishers.

Trademark notice: Product or corporate names may be trademarks or registered trademarks, and are used only for identification and explanation without intent to infringe.

British Library Cataloguing-in-Publication Data
A catalogue record for this book is available from the British Library

Library of Congress Cataloging-in-Publication Data
Names: Davis, Stephanie (Lecturer in critical psychology), author.
Title: Queer and trans people of colour in the UK : possibilities for intersectional richness / Stephanie Davis.
Identifiers: LCCN 2022036766 (print) | LCCN 2022036767 (ebook) | ISBN 9781138345768 (hardback) | ISBN 9781138345775 (paperback) | ISBN 9780429437694 (ebook) | ISBN 9780429794810 (adobe pdf) | ISBN 9780429794803 (epub) | ISBN 9780429794797 (mobi)
Subjects: LCSH: Gays—Great Britain. | Sexual minorities—Great Britain. | Transsexuals—Great Britain. | Intersectionality (Sociology)—Great Britain.
Classification: LCC HQ76.3.G7 D38 2023 (print) | LCC HQ76.3.G7 (ebook) | DDC 306.760941—dc23/eng/20220804
LC record available at https://lccn.loc.gov/2022036766
LC ebook record available at https://lccn.loc.gov/2022036767

ISBN: 978-1-138-34576-8 (hbk)
ISBN: 978-1-138-34577-5 (pbk)
ISBN: 978-0-429-43769-4 (ebk)

DOI: 10.4324/9780429437694

Typeset in Bembo
by codeMantra

CONTENTS

Acknowledgements ix

1 Introduction 1

2 Exploring QTPOC lives 21

3 Theorising multiplicity 32

4 A question of belonging 49

5 Building community 69

6 Decolonising sexuality and gender 85

7 Conflict and harm in community: the possibilities for the reparative and transformative 100

8 Conclusion 112

References 120
Index 129

ACKNOWLEDGEMENTS

The beginnings of this book can be traced back to Manchester in late 2012, early 2013 with a group of Black queer women deciding to make a space for themselves and to build community with other queer and trans people of colour. Thank you to those involved in co-founding Rainbow Noir, for co-creating a place with me that felt like home and through which I met a beautiful community and network of folks who showed me love, generosity, and the rich intersectional beauty of our queerness and transness of colour. A blessing and a gift.

Thank you to the queer and trans people of colour communities in the UK and those I have met across Europe for your creativity, commitment, and loving kindness in developing spaces, clubs, networks, festivals, and possibilities for belonging and community.

Thank you to my participants without whom this work would not have been possible, who shared and trusted me with their invaluable knowledge and understandings of what it means to be a queer and/or trans person of colour in the world. It has been wonderful to spend the last seven years 'thinking alongside'[1] your words and thoughts, they have enriched my life, and I hope they will do the same for others.

Thank you to the Egun (ancestors) who have blessed me with the fire in my spirit and rebellion in my bones whose fugitivity pushes me forward to continue to dream, imagine, create the possibilities for collective liberation and ways of being free in the world. Thank you to my Grandad, Jerzy Marchelewicz, and my Nan, Hyacinth Joyce Davis, who both passed during my academic training but whose lives were a testament to resistance to fascism and coloniality and taught me strength, boldness, love, and humour in the face of great difficulty.

Thank you to Linda and Gerald Davis for encouraging and loving my critical, or as Mum would call it 'contrary', thinking. Thank you for your emotional, financial, and practical support in completing the PhD and this monograph.

It's through your example I have learnt to find compassion, joy, and happiness even in the hardest of times.

Thank you Sophie Anderson-Davis, for your love and generosity, always being there to support me and for keeping me laughing along the way. Thank you both Sophie Anderson-Davis and Bobby Anderson for always welcoming me into your home as a place of warmth and respite from the difficulties of being an early career academic and in writing this book. Thank you to my niblings, you are pure love and light and you sleeping on my chest during writing breaks have been when I have known true peace and joy.

Thank you, Ellis J. Johnson, for your light, love and generosity, and your care in supporting me through some of the most difficult times. Thank you for always sparking the fires of spirit, nature, and growing and thinking more deeply, and for building our hive together.

Thank you to Katherine Johnson for encouraging the generous and reparative in my work, and sharing it as a way of being in the academy. Your continued support has been immeasurable, and I am incredibly grateful to consider you my friend as well as my mentor.

Thank you Chloe Cousins, Suriya Aisha, and Sabah Choudrey, for your commitment to QTPOC communities in the UK, sharing your thoughts on your work and life, and for your truest friendship.

Thank you Arlie Adlington, for your kindness, friendship, and support through some of the hardest times.

Thank you Rachel Jane Liebert and Tehseen Noorani for your warmth, encouragement, and conspiring together for the other-worldly possibilities of the borderlands.

Thank you Ali Lara and Sophia Bokhari, for your solidarity and friendship, and for creating our radical brown office as a haven in difficult circumstances.

Thank you Juno Mac and Dean Peters for your kindness and generosity.

Thank you Daniela De Armas and Ile Oshun Kayode for your spiritual guidance, connection, and keeping me on my path.

Thank you to my incredible team of doctoral supervisors – Katherine Johnson, Hannah Frith, and Nichola Khan, thank you for your commitment to and belief in my scholarship, my life is much richer from working with you all. Thank you for your generosity, kindness, and for teaching me so much.

Thank you to Gail Lewis and Meg-John Barker my external examiners for their valuable time, encouragement, and advice who continue to inspire me with their work and praxis.

Thank you Erica Burman, Ian Parker, and Elizabeth Peel, for offering a different path in psychology and the captivating possibilities of a critical psychology. Thank you for your encouragement in developing the early stages of my academic career at both undergraduate and postgraduate levels.

Thank you to the British Psychological Society's Psychology of Women and Equalities Section (BPS POWES) for nurturing my academic development and confidence and illuminating the possibilities of a critical and feminist psychology.

Thank you for the camaraderie, solidarity, laughter, and generosity. Thank you especially to Marcia Worrell, you are so very missed.

Thank you to Havva Mustafa and Catherine Wilson for your insights and holding space for me. Your emotional support has made me a better writer and thinker and made life more liveable and joyful.

Thank you Frantz Fanon, Ntozake Shange, and Alexis Pauline Gumbs for changing my life, creating beauty and poetry of the rich inner life-worlds of Black folk, and challenging us to face the question of the 'psycho-existential complex'[2] of being Black in a white world. Thank you for helping me to envision the possibilities and, hopefully, realities of scholar-activism committed to Black and brown lives and intersectional liberation. Black feminism is indeed the answer.[3]

Thank you to the University of Brighton Doctoral College for the studentship and funding to undertake this doctoral work.

Thank you to Routledge and the series editors – Katherine Johnson and Kath Browne – for your flexibility, time, and support in publishing the monograph.

Details of Research Participants

Participants for focus groups were drawn from three QTPOC activist and social groups across the UK:

'Brighton/London' group

This London-based group had had earlier iterations as a QTPOC group in Brighton, which now no longer exists and had come before Brighton Group 2. Group members had since moved to London and had started a London-based QTPOC group which has been running since 2011.

Brighton Group 2

This was a more recent QTPOC group that had separately developed in Brighton in 2014 a couple of years after the first group. Brighton is a coastal town in the South-East of England known for its large LGBTQ population and positioned as a LGBTQ weekend or holiday destination. It has a very small Black and brown community which is not very visible. Brighton Group 2 were a majority of young people under the age of 25, some were students and others worked in the town. As of December 2020, it is unclear if the group continues to meet and newer QTPOC groups have emerged in the city more recently.

Group X

This is a QTIPOC (Queer Trans Intersex People of Colour) group based in the North-West of England in a large town which is well known for its LGBTQ population and has a historically large population of Black and brown communities which continues to grow. Group X is diverse in its membership and compared to the other two groups in the research has a much more visible presence of members who were seeking asylum. Group X has been running since 2013.

Across the focus groups two-thirds of the participants were Black or Black/mixed race (of African descent), the rest were Arab and South Asian. The majority were cis women and four were trans and non-binary people. Their ages ranged from young people in their early twenties to those in their mid-forties. During the time of the research, there was limited visibility of intersex people within the QTPOC networks and none of the participants explicitly identified as intersex. At the time the acronym QTPOC was more widely used, and during the process of the research, groups began to include intersex explicitly in their naming.

Interviewees were drawn from the same three QTPOC groups and some had also been involved in the focus groups. Each interview participant was invited to write their own summary about themselves.

Ashok/a
Ashok/a is a Working Class, Brown, South Asian/Bengali, Bi, Queer, Trans, Genderfucker living in London. They are Disabled, Mad, a Survivor and a Benefits Claimant. They have been an organiser in feminist/queer/qtibpoc (Queer Trans Intersex Black People of Colour)/disability/mad communities and are in their 40s. They write, make art, and are trying to relearn bass guitar. Among their passions are art, music, fashion, food, cats, and liberation.

Janelle
Janelle is a 25-year-old cis queer femme of Arab origin, British-born, grown up and still identifies as Muslim. She works as a dentist full time but is involved in queer activism, and co-founded a social group for queer, trans and intersex people of colour in her current city of residence.

Kai
Kai is a mixed race non-binary trans person in their 30s. They grew up poor but got to Uni and through it by working full time for much of it. They have organised as an environmental and social justice activist in different parts of the country but most of their activism is focused on people of colour community organising, these days specifically QTIPOC organising.

Sasha
Sasha is a LGBT youth and community work coordinator and organiser and worker living and working in the North-West. Sasha is a 25-year-old cis woman, who identifies as gay/queer. She is of Black Caribbean and white British descent.

Stanley
Stanley is a mixed race trans man, academic and artist. He is of Black Caribbean and white Welsh and Irish working-class heritage. Stanley came of age in the 1980s and 90s and has been involved with trans and gender projects, giving many academic papers on childhood gender nonconformity both locally and in Europe, as well as contributing to transgender and queer publications, anthologies, and art exhibitions within the UK.

Notes

1 Kassem, A. (2021). Anti-Muslim Hate on the Eastern Shores of the Mediterranean: Lebanon, the Hijab, and Modernity/Coloniality. *Ethnic and Racial Studies, 1–21*, 2.
2 Fanon, F. (1986). *Black Skins, White Masks* (p. 14). London: Pluto Press.
3 Brown, A., and Brown, A.M. (Hosts). (2017, December 19). A Breathing Chorus with Alexis Pauline Gumbs. [Audio podcast episode]. In *How to Survive the End of the World*. https://www.endoftheworldshow.org/?offset=1519744850304.

1
INTRODUCTION

Introduction

Over the last ten years in the UK we have seen the emergence of networks of Black and brown[1] lesbian, gay, bisexual, trans, and queer (LGBTQ) activists and groups, operating in spaces distinct from mainstream LGBTQ organisations and activists. These include activist and social group spaces, as well as community events such as Black Pride and the Cutie BIPoC (Black, Indigenous, and People of Colour) Berlin Festival (of which some organisers and attendees are UK based), art collectives and club nights such as Pxssy Palace and Bootylicious in London, Urban Slag in Birmingham, and Akbar Umm and Chew Disco in Manchester.

Concomitantly LGBT rights have moved from the margins to become a central concern for modern politics in the UK. Increasingly 'openness to sexual diversity' has been 'hailed as ... quintessential feature of Western societies' (Colpani and Habed, 2014, p. 73). The UK Conservative government has positioned itself as a champion for LGB rights, noting its recent legislative, 'progressive' gains for LGBT people against a recent historical backdrop of homophobic party policies (Lawrence and Taylor, 2020). However, despite recent 'unprecedented' progress for LGBT people in the UK, there remains 'enduring stasis, where particular issues (and lives) are rendered immobile as perennial "sticking points" and, in the words of Penny Mordaunt MP, as issues "too tough" to address' (Lawrence and Taylor, 2020, p. 588).

Lawrence and Taylor (2020) question 'linear conceptions of progress of inevitably and uniformly "getting better"', noting that 'tensions cyclically re-emerge' around gender and sexuality (p. 599). As legal rights have progressed there are ongoing battles around LGBT youth provision, inclusive sex and relationships education, the rights of LGBT asylum seekers, and reforming the Gender

DOI: 10.4324/9780429437694-1

Recognition Act (GRA) alongside systemic queerphobia and transphobia. There is strong resistance to trans rights, encouraged by supposed feminist activists and politicians, among both right- and left-wing media and legitimised through the government's own hostility towards trans and gender diverse people's self-definition (Hines, 2019; Lawrence and Taylor, 2020). Lawrence and Taylor (2020) highlight that in the government's own LGBT Action Plan, launched in 2018, there is a pathologising emphasis on trans youth and the "impact" of transition in particular for trans and gender diverse youth who were "assigned female at birth" (GEO, 2018a: 9, cited in Lawrence and Taylor, 2020, p. 599). This emphasis 'implicitly legitimises' anti-trans and so-called 'gender critical' rhetoric which positions trans and gender diverse experience as a form of 'social contagion' (p. 599).

The narrative of LGBT inclusion and legal progressiveness can be critiqued by highlighting these 'significant', 'entrenched', and 'galvanising' resistances to LGBT equality and ongoing inequality in the UK (Browne and Nash, 2014, pp. 323, 327). However, it must also be critiqued for the ways in which LGBT[2] inclusion has been operationalised as part of what Puar (2007) has called the homonationalist project. These are the neo-colonial ways in which the Global North has utilised LGBT rights to position itself as progressive against the 'uncivilized' Global South, drawing specific types of LGBT subject into a 'homonormative' citizenship and investment in the nation state. Puar (2008, p. 2) argues that the 'ascendancy' of LGBT inclusion and rights is 'contingent' upon specific 'racial politics'; that the development of LGBT rights in the West is 'concurrent' and dependent upon 'less progressive discourses concerning immigration, race and international relations, such as the war on terror in the USA, or the failure of multiculturalism in the UK' (Raboin, 2017, p. 664). Raboin (2017, p. 665) notes how LGBT rights sit 'precariously between the global pursuit of LGBTI equality and an ongoing civilizing mission'. LGBT rights have been utilised as a tool for defining the racialised, colonised Other and the question of their belonging in the UK and in the need for their 'education' in the Global South. This homonationalist discourse sets up the Global North as the "saviour" of sexual and gender diverse people of the Global South and can be seen to impose Western-centric understandings of sexual identity, behaviour, and embodiment (Browne and Nash, 2014).

At the same time queerphobia and transphobia remain entrenched in the UK, and trans rights are subject to ongoing hostilities – with vitriol towards the 'authenticity' of trans women as women and significant backlash over proposals to legally recognise an individual's right to self-determine their gender (Hines, 2019, p. 10; Pearce et al., 2020). Tudor (2021, p. 239) notes the alignment of 'gender critical' and 'radical feminists' with 'anti-gender and far-right anti-immigration rhetoric' which characterises the GRA as 'fostering sexual violence' – suggesting that the GRA will allow 'men' to pretend they are women to access women-only space to do harm. The spectre of the trans woman as sexual predator is reminiscent of the figure of the racialised other, from which white cis women must be protected. This works on colonial, binary constructions of gender and of womanhood as cis, white, and vulnerable to attacks by the Other, occluding patriarchal violence and continuing the dehumanisation of the colonised and those who do not fit the binary (Tudor, 2021). Struggle against these current attacks by transphobic feminists and the far right can find solidarity with the continued Black feminist and decolonial struggle against coloniality, white universal conceptualisations of womanhood, and indeed gender itself (Snorton, 2017).

Contrasting the 'progression' of LGBT movements in the UK within this complex political climate with the emergence of Black and brown LGBTQ activist networks raises questions about the inclusion of Black and brown LGBTQ populations within LGBTQ movements. Specifically, what is the meaning of these activist groups for those involved, how might these spaces support Black and brown LGBTQ people to navigate the wider political context, and how they are positioned within them and what can their lived experiences tell us about modern LGBTQ movements and British society more widely? To understand this, we must also understand the place of Black and brown populations in Britain and the specific British histories of immigration in a post-colonial context.

From my own practice as a community organiser and continuing involvement in these activist groups, there is also a question of Black and brown LGBTQ inclusion within wider so-called Black and brown communities, third sector organisations, and activist networks. The position of Black and brown LGBTQ people within LGBTQ and Black and brown communities raises issues of the intersections of race, gender, and sexuality; belonging; and how individuals and communities negotiate these possible tensions. *Queer and Trans People of Colour in the UK: Possibilities for Intersectional Richness* is an in-depth examination of the meaning of these networks for those involved and what this collective work provides for individual subjectivity and identity. The explicitly activist and social support group networks that are the focus of this book self-define as 'queer and trans people of colour' or 'QTPOC' and this term will be used to refer to these groups and their members.

The term 'QTPOC' is described by UK activists as:

> Queers are: Intersex, Bisexual, Transgender, Lesbian, Gay, Queer, Gender-Queer, Gender-Variant or non-conforming, Undefined, Questioning, and Exploring persons.
>
> Of colour: Those who are descended (through one or more parents) anywhere in Africa, Asia, the Middle East, Indigenous peoples of Australasia, the Americas, the Islands of the Atlantic, Indian Pacific, and Roma Sinti (and) Travellers. We explicitly welcome and invite mixed heritage people. Our group includes people with varied race, ethnicity, and sexual and gender identities. We welcome anyone who self-identifies as both queer and persons (people) of colour.
>
> *(Taken from the QTIPOC [Queer, Trans, Intersex People of Colour] London Facebook group page)*

The term 'people of colour' has emerged from the US context and its uptake in the UK is a move away from the use of 'political Blackness', which developed within British histories of anti-racist struggle in the 1970s onwards. Political Blackness brought together recent immigrants to Britain from the British Commonwealth, most notably those from South Asia and the African Caribbean, developing a Black consciousness uniting those who experienced the brunt of colonialism and racism. Most importantly, this encouraged solidarity work in resistance to the racist oppression of the British state.

Mehmood (2008, p. 5) describes Black as a *political* colour that could only exist in a white world'. Political Blackness continues to be used by some communities and activists today; however, it continues to be a fiercely contested term. The definition used by QTIPOC London of 'people of colour' is utilised across many QTPOC groups in the UK and by all groups involved in this study. However, the definition of 'people of colour' used by the organisers of QTIPOC London is based on a definition of politically Black by the Black Lesbian and Gay Centre that had existed in Peckham, London, in the 1980s. This ties the contemporaneous network of QTPOC activism to the histories of Black (both politically Black and of African descent) lesbian and gay activism in the 1980s and 1990s across the UK.

In this work, I move between the use of the terms Lesbian, Gay, Bisexual, Trans, Queer (LGBTQ), Queer and Trans People of Colour (QTPOC), Black (of African descent), Black (political Blackness), brown, Asian, and Arab depending on the different social/political/historical contexts I am referring to, the use of different terms in previous research, and the preference of participants. It should be noted that participants used several different terms for their own personal identities as well as positioning themselves under the umbrella of QTPOC.

The book focuses on the possible tensions within LGBTQ and Black and brown communities for QTPOC within the specific British post-colonial context alongside the changing political conditions for LGBTQ people. I examine how QTPOC activist networks provide space for the negotiation of these possible tensions; the intersections of racism, queerphobia, and transphobia and marginalisation; questions of belonging; and the multiplicity of subjectivity.

This addresses several gaps in the wider literature. First, much of the previous research has been undertaken within the US context and there is a lack of understanding of the specificities of the British context. Second, the small amount of research in psychology on the intersections of race, sexuality, and gender takes a deficit approach – focusing only on the problems of being multiply minoritised and failing to take account of the ways resistance and collective action forge new possibilities and subjectivities for QTPOC (Akerlund and Cheung, 2000). Third, psychology is limited in its understanding of intersectionality and historical, political, and social contexts, lacking much theoretical and empirical work on race and its intersections and the lived experiences of Black and brown people in the UK.

I take a critical psychological approach, exploring how QTPOC subjectivities are shaped by wider social, historical, and political contexts while also considering how QTPOC collectivism may provide forms of resistance to multiple oppression and isolation, further shaping subjectivity.

Utilising the critical theory of Black feminist, anti-/post-/de-colonial, and queer theory, I examine the intertwining and co-construction of race, gender, and sexuality – specifically using the theory of intersectionality to understand how subjects are interpellated through intersecting processes of racialisation, gender, and sexualisation. Building on the work of Fanon (1986), Mama (1995), Butler (1997), Lewis (2000), Phoenix (2013), and Nayak (2015) in and outside of critical psychology, I consider how post-colonial, racist, sexist, queerphobic, and transphobic social structures may structure the psyche and subjectivity, how they are 'inverted' back onto the self and others, and resisted and contested through collectivised political action (Rassool, 1997, p. 195). This will be framed within the wider post-colonial context of QTPOC specifically in the UK, and how QTPOC are positioned within mainstream political rhetoric which has embraced the language of women's and LGB(T?) people's rights as a part of British exceptionalism and liberalism.

Situating QTPOC within histories of struggle in the UK

Before exploring QTPOC activism and subjectivities further, it is critically important to briefly trace and situate QTPOC within histories of Black and brown immigrant political organising in Britain. It is important to note that I can only provide a brief and partial history due to the limits of this book. These histories are important in understanding the lived experience of being an 'ethnic minority' in Britain and to consider how multiply minoritised identities and subjectivities are shaped within the context of political consciousness, collective action, and resistance.

South Asians, West Africans, African Caribbeans and African Americans have long and multiple histories of political organising in the UK; resisting colonialism, imperialism, and racism; and shaping British Black and brown subjectivities (Hesse, 2000; Boyce Davies, 2008; Ramamurthy, 2013). Hesse (2000, p. 99) is critical of the popular narratives which claim the 1948 Windrush era of immigration to be the 'originary' moment for African and Caribbean communities in the UK and for Black British subjectivity. This narrative occludes the existence of African, Caribbean, and African American sea-faring communities in the UK from the 1830s onwards in places such as Liverpool, Cardiff, and London. Hesse (2000, p. 103) argues that the 'continuity of this development into the twentieth century became part of the outward looking formation of [for example] Black Liverpool anchored in pre-Windrush, regionalized, urban Black affinity with some of the diasporic lineages of the Atlantic world'.

Pre-Windrush Britain was a centre of Black [of African descent] political action with Pan-Africanist and anti-colonial organising, with visits from many anti-colonial activists such as Kwame Nkrumah, Nnamdi Azikiwe, C.L.R. James, George Padmore, Jomo Kenyatta, and Amy Jacques Garvey. This work developed within the 'overlapping discourses of the African diaspora, the British

Empire, anti-colonialism, decolonisation, migration, Black settlement and British nationalism' (p. 103). Several anti-colonial, Pan-Africanist campaigning organisations emerged in the UK in the 1920s and 1930s such as the West African Students Union, the League of Coloured People (LCP), the International African Services Bureau (IASB), and the Pan-African Federation, and in 1945 the fifth Pan-African Congress was held in Manchester. Hesse (2000) argues that these histories are integral to understanding the emergence of political Blackness and the development of Black [of African descent] British subjectivity, of a diasporic consciousness in specific 'regionalized' Black experiences rooted in Pan-Africanist, anti-imperial, and anti-colonial discourses.

Boyce Davies (2008) illustrates how the work of African and Caribbean activists, such as Claudia Jones in the 1950s, helped to develop Black British forms of subjectivity and identity through the establishment of Notting Hill Carnival and other cultural forms. This work was a form of 'cultural affirmation', supporting the development of a post-colonial African and Caribbean diasporic consciousness and subjectivity, cementing 'black solidarity and … inter-racial friendship' (p. 173). This work created space for '"new associations which were being formed" and play[ed] a role in the definition of African-Caribbean identity in Britain, replacing the earlier "British colonial subject" identity that many of the immigrants carried with them to the United Kingdom' (p. 173). These connected immigrants to ongoing anti-colonial and anti-imperial struggles on the African continent and in the Caribbean, as well as the opportunity for organised resistance against racist discrimination in housing, employment, health care, and education in Britain. Black solidarity also supported the struggle against racist violence on the streets of the UK.

Similarly, Ramamurthy (2013) notes the long history of South Asian political organising in Britain which called for Indian independence as well as addressing South Asian workers' rights in Britain. The Workers Welfare League of India was set up in 1916 by Shapurji Saklatvala of the Communist Party, the Lascar's Welfare League and the Indian Seaman's Association were set up in the 1920s, and Indian Workers' Associations (IWAs) were established in the 1930s. After Indian independence in 1947 the IWAs went into decline; however, these were re-established in the 1950s in areas in the UK with large Punjabi populations – to address both post-colonial struggles in India as well as addressing racial discrimination, such as the 'colour bar in housing' in Britain and being 'forced to accept the lowest paid, most dangerous jobs and unsociable working hours' (pp. 11, 13; Josephides, 1991). In facing social exclusion, more informal organising developed to share resources among 'extended families and former village networks' (Ramamurthy, 2013, p. 11).

As both Hesse (2000) and Ramamurthy (2013) suggest, these early forms of African, Caribbean, and South Asian political activism in Britain laid the foundations for the development of 'political Blackness' from the 1960s onwards in 'resistance against the rising tide of racism and fascism' (Ramamurthy, 2013, p. 12). Black became a 'political colour', a form of inter- and intra-racial solidarity (Sivanandan, 1983, p. 3).

Sivanandan (1983, p. 2) describes the 1962 Commonwealth Immigration Act as the point at which racism 'begins to get institutionalised', and in which immigration becomes and remains a key policy issue for all the main political parties through to the present day. The 1960s saw the 'nationalisation' of racism, 'crystallised in [Enoch] Powell's 1968 "Rivers of Blood" speech' with increasing violent, racist attacks on immigrant communities (Ramamurthy, 2013, pp. 11/12). These attacks and murders were 'not simply perpetrated by gangs on the street but also by the police and state institutions' such as in the murder of David Oluwale, a Nigerian stowaway, in Leeds at the hands of two police officers in April 1968 following years of 'hounding' by the police and mental health services (Aspden, 2008, p. 1; Ramamurthy, 2013, p. 13).

The intensification of racial discrimination and violence called for more vigorous resistance, and with the seeds sown from previous anti-colonial and anti-racist work, African, Caribbean, and South Asian solidarity work developed through the project of political Blackness. Sivanandan (1983) describes political Blackness as a 'community and a class ... we closed ranks and took up each other's struggles' (p. 3). Mirza (1997) expressed that political Blackness in Britain was about 'a state of "becoming" (racialized); a process of consciousness' (p. 3). In being 'located through your "otherness", a "conscious coalition" emerges: a self-consciously constructed space where identity is not inscribed by a natural identification but a political kinship' (p. 3). Therefore, 'to be black in Britain is to share a common structural location; a racial location' (p. 3). The project of political Blackness supported the 'shared experience of objectification', making sense of place in a white world and importantly building resistance through 'politicized collective action' (p. 3). This created space for the possibility of new forms of Black, both politically Black and of African descent, radical subjectivities (Mama, 1995).

In the 1960s and 1970s burgeoning Black Power and Asian Youth Movements espoused the right to self-defence for politically Black communities, campaigning for Black rights, against immigration laws, and 'building a rich infrastructure of organisations, parties, and self-help projects' (Sivanandan, 1983, p. 3). Parties included the United People's Alliance, the Black Unity and Freedom Party, the Black Liberation Front, and the Black Panthers, all of whom had their own 'projects, newspapers, news-sheets, schools' (p. 3).

Organisations developed their own strike committees who would travel to different strikes offering support and learning from one another from the differing but also similar traditions of anti-colonial resistance. Sivanandan (1983, p. 3) describes the 'weaving' of contemporary and past struggles of resistance from across the colonies, including Ireland, the Commonwealth, and Black Power in the US as creating a 'beautiful massive texture that in turn strengthened the struggles here and fed back to the struggles there'. The weaving of these struggles can be understood to shape political Black subjectivities, as Rassool (1997, p. 188) notes that Black identity and subjectivity 'are not linear constructions but rather they reflect a tapestry of interwoven life experiences having their origins within different socio-historical epochs'.

Black subjectivities are 'continually being shaped in their everyday interaction with the social world and thus they are flexible and engaged in a constant, reflexive, process of "becoming"' (p. 189). The history and legacies of political Blackness are therefore important to consider in the shaping of Black, brown and 'of colour' subjectivities. However, Sivanandan (1983) cites the recession in the 1970s and the Immigration Act of 1971 as a point at which the project of political Blackness began to be undermined. Different communities began to have different priorities. South Asian communities struggled against the tightening of immigration controls, 'arbitrary arrests and deportation' focusing on legal defences which led to a less coordinated approach (p. 4). African Caribbean communities, on the other hand, became more focused on the 'Sus' laws and the 'criminalisation of their young, police brutality and judicial bias' (p. 4). The 'Sus' law was the colloquial term for Stop and Search under section 4 of the Vagrancy Act 1824 which allowed police officers to stop and search:

> every suspected person or reputed thief, frequenting any river, canal, or navigable stream, dock, or basin, or any quay, wharf, or warehouse near or adjoining thereto, or any street, highway, or avenue leading thereto, or any place of public resort, or any avenue leading thereto, or any street… or any highway or any place adjacent to a street or highway; … with intent to commit … an … arrestable offence.
> *(Quote from: https://www.legislation.gov.uk/ukpga/Geo4/5/83)*

The Sus law was seen to disproportionately affect Black (of African descent) communities and was seen to be a causal factor in the early 1980s uprisings across major cities in England. These important struggles meant in part that 'priorities became separated' and the rich infrastructure that had been built up began to be 'eroded' (pp. 3/4). At the same time, the state's emphasis on *ethnicity* and state funding for community projects based on cultural difference 'de-linked black struggle', separating out different communities coalesced under political Blackness according to ethnic group (p. 4; Brah, 1996). Activists were co-opted into working on state-funded community projects, which worked to an extent to neutralise the project of political Blackness. However, Sivanandan (1983) notes that it was the Black women's movement that managed to continue much of the Black infrastructure from the 1970s to the 1990s, with a few lasting until the present day.

Throughout the 1970s Black women were beginning to demand the importance of addressing the intersections of gender and race in politically Black spaces as well as the women's liberation movement (Mason-John and Khambatta, 1993). Through 'ideological blind spots', attending to race, gender, and class separately, Mirza (1997, p. 4) describes Black women as occupying 'a location whose very nature resists telling'. Black British feminisms have sought to speak to the gendered experience of racialisation within 'patriarchal, colonial and now postcolonial discourse' and 'contest, and resist racist logics and practices in the everyday lives of black people' (pp. 5/6).

Introduction 9

The Black British feminist movement campaigned for the rights of immigrant women who were only formally able to 'claim rights on the grounds of marriage'; against sexual and domestic violence; supporting 'anti-colonial struggle'; supporting women's labour struggles; sit-ins against 'virginity tests' for Asian immigrant women; reproductive rights, challenging the use of Depo Provera and the forced sterilisation of Black women; to resist racist politics and harassment by the state and police; in 'defence campaigns' for those arrested in the 1981 uprisings; anti-deportation protests and 'challenging imperial feminism' (Mirza, 1997, pp. 7/10). Black women's organisations prospered in this time, and these included, among others, Liverpool Black Sisters, Muslim Women's Organisation, Manchester Black Women's Co-operative (Abasindi Co-op), Brixton Black Women's Group, Organisation of Women of African and Asian Descent (OWAAD), Southall Black Sisters, and Zanu Women's League.

As with political Blackness more generally, Mama (1995) argues the Black feminist movement and particularly the work of OWAAD led to the development of 'new cultural forms and articulations of identity' (p. 5). Similarly, Lewis (2000, p. 155) notes that 'challenges to the forms of thinking, knowledges and practices which articulate sexual, "racial" and other forms of difference have also provided the terrain upon which new political subjects and constituencies have been formed'. Mama (1995, p. 6) argues that the Black feminist 'articulation of Black identities was about changing one's consciousness of one's position in the world, about constructing new subjectivities and rejecting the disempowering legacies of centuries'.

Mama (1995, p. 100) identified two discourses that shaped her participants' subjectivities – a 'colonial-integrationist discourse and black radical discourse'. The colonial–integrationist discourse was a hegemonic discourse which encouraged assimilation and integration into the colonial or British 'dominant order' while the Black radical discourse encouraged 'a politics of resistance and subversion' (p. 100). Black radicalism has provided 'innovative and creative' theory and practice for resistance, such as Garveyism, nationalism, Rastafarianism, Negritude, Black Power, Black feminism, and political Blackness (p. 107). OWAAD can also be situated within this history of Black radicalism.

Research on Black women's subjectivities highlights dis-identificatory strategies to subvert racist, sexist oppression – that they were and are not merely 'passive recipients' (Rassool, 1997, p. 191; Munoz, 1999). I draw on Munoz's (1999) concept of dis-identification here alongside Mama's (1995, p. 117) research in which she considers the 'coexistence of subject positions and the ... multiplicity of subjectivity'. Mama (1995) highlights the contradictory ways in which subjectivity is formed through identification with both colonial–integrationist and Black radical discourses. Munoz (1999, p. 12) adds to this tension the process of dis-identification – arguing that minority subjects do not simply assimilate or resist but that a third alternative emerges which is dis-identificatory in which the subject 'tactically and simultaneously works on, with and against a cultural form'. For Munoz (1999, p. 4) dis-identification is then 'meant to be descriptive of the survival strategies the minority subject practices in order to negotiate a phobic majoritarian public sphere that continuously elides or punishes the existence of subjects who do not conform'.

Mama's (1995, p. 6) theory of subjectivity was informed by the study of the 'ongoing process of cultural and individual change, change that was happening simultaneously within individuals and at the collective, social level' for Black British women within Black (of African descent) liberation and feminist movements. Post-colonial politically Black British subjectivities were always on the way, in the 'process of "becoming"' while managing the complexity of the 'interweaving of "past-present"' (Rassool, 1997, pp. 188/189). It should be understood that this process of becoming is a 'contradictory process' given that Black and brown people 'have been brought into Britain, and yet the history of their presence continuously denied' (Mama, 1995, p. 95).

Black feminist organising highlighted the need to address the intersections of political Blackness, addressing the lived experience of those who were minoritised within a minority. However, within some of these organisations the intersections of race, gender, and *sexuality* were a painful topic of contention (Carmen et al., 1984). The treatment of Black lesbians at OWAAD's 1981 conference and the division over a lesbian discussion group on the schedule 'contributed' to the folding of the organisation the following year (Mason-John and Khambatta, 1993, p. 12). Despite this, the 1980s saw an 'explosion' of events for Black lesbians in London, and elsewhere in the country parties in people's homes called 'Blues, with a DJ, bar, and door charge, were the only meeting places for many Black lesbians' (p. 13).

In comparison to the small number of contemporary QTPOC networks a huge number of Black gay and lesbian groups and organisations developed throughout the 1980s such as the Gay Asian Group, which later became the Lesbian and Gay Black Group, which founded the Black Lesbian and Gay Centre (in Peckham, London), Black Lesbian Group, Chinese Lesbian Group, Shakti for South Asian lesbians and gay men, Latin American Lesbian Group, Lesbians and Policing Project (LESPOP), Young Black Zami's, Black Lesbians Brought Up In Care Group, Black MESMAC Project (Safer Sex project for Black men), MOSAIC for lesbians and gay men of mixed race heritage, Lesbian and Gay Immigration Group, Black Lesbians and Gay People of Faith, the Black Pervert's Network (Private parties for Black and Asian men), and the Iranian Lesbian and Gay Group (Mason-John and Khambatta, 1993; See rukus! federation).

In 1985 Zami I, the first British Black Lesbian conference, was held in London with over 200 women of African and Asian descent attending. A second Zami conference was held in Birmingham in 1989. To note, Zami is

> a Caribbean word particular to the island of Carriacou. The late Audre Lorde in her book Zami: A New Spelling of My Name (1982) uses zami to describe women who have sexual and loving relationships with each other. Since then some black women have used zami to define their sexual preference.
>
> *(Mason-John and Khambatta, 1993, p. 38)*

The first national Black Gay Men's Conference, 'In This Our Lives', was held in London in 1987.

These organisations and networks worked to support those multiply minoritised within Black (politically and of African descent), women, and lesbian and gay movements and communities; campaigned and gave advice on issues of immigration from a lesbian and gay perspective; challenged homophobia in Black media and culture; developed publishing houses for Black lesbian literature; and created media and culture such as *Outwrite* which was an 'anti-racist, anti-imperialist' monthly paper which discussed lesbian lives across the world (Mason-John, 1995, p. 18). The group 'Wages Due Lesbians' (WDL) was an example of Black lesbians and white lesbians working together in solidarity in anti-racist struggle, with the main aim of reparations for lesbians (and all women) to be 'compensated for their unrecognized work' (p. 18). WDL fought for 'the Black woman not to be torn between her Black and lesbian identity, and … highlighted the link between homophobia, poverty and economic exploitation' (p. 18). WDL supported campaigns for the rights of lesbian mothers; campaigns against Section 28 which banned literature and discussion about lesbian and gay people in schools and local authorities in the UK from 1988 to 2003; and the testing of AZT (an experimental drug for HIV) on HIV-positive African children (p. 19). Both politically Black and Black of African descent lesbian and gay organisations overlapped with the struggles of the Black feminist and the wider Black liberation movements linking the international with the national and local, supporting anti-imperialist and anti-colonial work and issues facing Black communities in the UK. However, as inferred by the proliferation of support groups and the work of the WDL these organisations also addressed the *existentialist* dilemma of being multiply minoritised through race, gender, and sexuality and their intersections.

Unfortunately, most of the Black women's and lesbian and gay organisations, projects and networks had folded by the mid-1990s. Mason-John and Khambatta (1993) note how much of this work was supported financially by progressive Labour local authorities in the early 1980s, particularly the Greater London Council (GLC); however, many were 'sceptical' about working with local government (p. 17). This is echoed by Sivanandan's (1983) concerns of co-option of more radical work into liberal institutions. The risks of being funded by local authorities also came to fruition in the late 1980s when Section 28 of the Local Government Act of 1988 was passed by a Conservative government. By the end of the 1980s 'lesbian and gay, women's, disability and race units were being dismantled' (Mason-John and Khambatta, 1993, p. 17). The severity of funding cuts, unemployment, and 'repressive immigration measures' disproportionately affected Black communities, particularly Black women and gay men and lesbians, who had been buoyed by the increased attention to equalities in the 1980s (p. 18). The difficulty of sustaining community organisations and networks put activists under huge pressures, leaving many 'burnt out or demoralised' often with no-one else able to take up the mantle (Mason-John, 1995, p. 49). The 'plethora' of groups that had once existed were diminished into 'fragmented networks', with many groups turning to organise around ethnicity with little emphasis on 'building alliances' (Mason-John and Khambatta, 1993, p. 18). By the beginning of the 1990s many felt that they had lost the original sense of community.

QTPOC groups must be situated within these very recent and past histories of struggle. In fact, members of some of these groups include original members of the Black lesbian and gay groups from the 1980s. In considering the recent development of QTPOC networks in the UK, we must contemplate the place of these groups in how they shape new forms of political subjectivities for those who continue to be positioned as outsiders to Britain and Europe, and in relation to progressive changes in the mainstream political rhetoric around women and LGBT equalities.

The Black feminist and the Black lesbian and gay movements of the 1970s onwards began the political work of complicating Black subjectivities in public, raising the issue of intersectionality and multiplicity, and contesting Black heteronormativity and 'authenticity' (Wright, 2013, p. 4). Wright (2013) has described the problematic of 'authenticity' in Black (of African descent) diasporic cultures which create hierarchies of authenticity – most commonly with the Black cisgender heterosexual man at the top of this hierarchy. Africa is positioned as the seat of Black authenticity, which creates a 'signifying chain that does in fact suggest that some Blacks are less "authentic" than others' (Wright, 2013, p. 6). A heteronormative lens is used to define authenticity, suggesting queer and trans Black people are somehow less authentically Black. This perpetuates 'anti-Black racist myths' (Wright, 2013, p. 6). Black feminist and Black lesbian and gay movements have had to navigate 'Black heteropatriarchal' ideology within Black Nationalist, Pan-Africanist, and some parts of Black Power movements as well as within wider Black communities, which seek to exclude them (Wright, 2013, p. 14).

Ward (2005, p. 493) describes Black churches in the US as 'directly and indirectly ... fostering homophobia'. He suggests several different root causes of homophobia within Black churches, pointing to the need to contextualise this phenomenon within the history of Black oppression in the US and the African continent. Ward (2005, p. 495) considers the centrality of literal interpretations of the Bible in Black churches as an issue which reinforces homophobia, and that this is shaped by a history of 'refuge and ... freedom in the literalness of Scripture' found by enslaved Black people.

Ward (2005, p. 496) also puts forward the theory that silence around sexuality within Black communities can be understood as a 'psycho-cultural response to the history of white exploitation of black sexuality during slavery'. This is a continuing fear of the white gaze and the history of racialised–sexualised stereotypes of Black people – such as the animalistic sexuality of the 'African', the promiscuous Jezebel, and the hypersexual, predatory Black man which continue to have material consequences. The fear of Black sexuality as already being seen to be queer and perverse may lead Black communities to be silent and self-disciplining when it comes to public discussions of sex and sexuality.

Third, Ward (2005) considers the 'melding' of Black Nationalist ideology, which suggests that the Black race will be liberated through the centring of Black masculinity and patriarchy, alongside the ideology of traditional Christianity and its homophobia. This has meant that whiteness and homosexuality have been regarded as 'weakness and femininity' while Black masculinity has 'been constructed in hyper masculine terms' – that it is the place of the (heterosexual, cisgender) Black man that needs to be affirmed to ensure the continuation and liberation of the Black 'race' (p. 495). Homophobia could be understood to be 'used as a strategy of domination', to affirm Black men within a wider social context within which they are disempowered (p. 497). This of course has potential emotional consequences for Black LGBT people as well as heterosexual and cisgender Black people. There have been similar tensions within other Black and brown communities, and this is a pressure which QTPOC also must negotiate.

The wider histories and legacies of politically Black, Black (of African descent), and brown histories of struggle have laid the foundations for understanding the 'central role that colonialism/neo-colonialism, diaspora, ethnic "Otherness" and the development of cultural hybridity have played in the shaping of ... subjectivities' of Black[3] and brown people in the UK (Rassool, 1997, p. 192).

It is critically important to situate QTPOC within these historical, social, and political contexts. *Queer and Trans People of Colour in the UK: Possibilities for Intersectional Richness* aims to understand what QTPOC groups mean for their members. It also seeks to explore how QTPOC have come to understand themselves as subjects through '(post)-colonial legacies'; the intersection of race, gender, and sexuality; alongside questions of belonging within LGBT and Black and brown communities and wider British society (Phoenix, 2013, p. 102).

This book is the first of its kind to consider the collective action of QTPOC activist groups in the UK, how this may shape individual subjectivities and living with multiplicity. I now turn to the limited previous research literature on QTPOC.

Reviewing the social science research into QTPOC

There is a lack of research on QTPOC in the UK, and particularly within psychology. There is a gap in understanding how subjectivities are formed for those living in multiplicity, and how in particular the intersections of race, gender, and sexuality are experienced. However, there is a small amount of empirical research literature on QTPOC in the North American and Canadian context and across other disciplines, such as sociology and public health. Much of the literature is focused on Black African and Caribbean queer men and HIV/public health, focusing on risk behaviours as 'men who have sex with men' or 'MSM' rather than issues of subjectivity (Clemon et al., 2012; Millet et al., 2012). However, in this literature there are discussions of individual behaviours and how these may be impacted by social contexts such as poverty, racism, homophobia, and a lack of social support.

Social support is a key issue; however, further research is needed into how QTPOC already negotiate these social contexts and lack of support from the multiple communities of which they are a part – from the tensions of homophobia and heteronormativity within Black and brown communities and racism and exclusion from LGBTQ communities.

The small amount of psychological literature on QTPOC research is themed around issues of identities and experiences of stress, resilience, and oppression in the US. Meyer (2003, p. 2) notes that LGB people have higher rates of mental illness, substance misuse, and suicide and explanations for this focus on 'stigma, prejudice, and discrimination' which create hostile environments for 'stigmatized minority groups'. Similarly, Kulick, Wernick, Woodford, and Renn (2017, p. 1125) note that people of colour[4] are 'at disproportionate risk for depression' and other mental illness in comparison to white communities. Meyer (2003, p. 2) calls this the 'minority stress' model. Meyer (2003) emphasises the interaction of stress and resilience. Meyer (2010, pp. 1, 2) raises the issue of the intersection of race and sexuality and the 'question of stress and resilience' – querying whether 'double' or triple minority status means QTPOC are more at 'risk' or possibly more resilient. Kulick et al. (2017, p. 1126) find research suggests LGBT people of colour experience 'unique forms of marginalisation' and therefore possibly 'increased rates of psychological distress'. Cyrus (2017, p. 197) argues that LGBT people of colour may experience 'excess stress' in negotiating intersecting minoritised race, gender, and sexuality statuses. For example, at the level of the group QTPOC may experience 'vicarious trauma' through witnessing attacks and discrimination experienced by other QTPOC – the individual is reminded of the constant risks and threats to themselves (Dominguez, 2017, p. 212). Sadika, Wiebe, Morrison, and Morrison (2020, p. 111) note how QTPOC experience 'intersectional microaggressions' from their families and communities of colour as well as within majority white LGBTQ spaces. However, they noted a complex picture regarding relationships within communities of colour – some participants experienced affirming relationships within their communities of colour, while others felt a sense of 'disconnection' from family and friends of colour (p. 133).

Hailey, Burton, and Arscott (2020) point to the increased risk of experiencing pernicious social and psychological outcomes for African American LGBTQ youth in comparison to white heterosexuals due to the intersections of white supremacy, queerphobia, and transphobia. This can be traumatising and lead to long-term poorer health outcomes. This can be understood as 'complex trauma' referring to the simultaneous experiences of stress of the daily processes of minoritisation and structural inequalities which limit 'opportunities for wellbeing and positive development' (Kulick et al., 2017, p. 1127).

The 'resilience hypothesis' suggests that for Black LGBTQ people because of their experiences of racism they may have more resilience to manage this excess stress because of their access to Black communities in which they have strategies to protect their mental health from the everyday experiences of racism (Cyrus, 2017, p. 197). This might help them deal with stress related to queerphobia and transphobia. However, on the other hand the theory of resilience suggests that LGBTQ people of colour have more resources to manage minority stress because of their pre-existing and lifelong struggle with racism and white supremacy.

However, Cyrus (2017) points out that generally minoritised groups have less access to resources to address stress – therefore the resilience hypothesis may not clarify LGBTQ people of colour's experiences. Cyrus (2017, p. 200) argues that we must explore the ways in which LGBTQ people of colour 'achieve "success"' and consider 'variations of resilience' to deepen our understanding of stress and resilience. We require creative explorations as to how QTPOC navigate these complexities. This might include exploring the positive psychological benefits of 'non-familial kinship communities' or chosen families which may buffer rejection by biological families (Hailey, Burton, and Arscott, 2020, p. 177).

There is some exploration as to how QTPOC conceptualise their multiple identities; some research has looked at how QTPOC may develop cohesive identities, whereas other research has conceptualised identities in relation to public and private space (e.g. Hunter, 2010; Clemon et al., 2012). However, Meyer (2012) warns against dichotomising racial and sexual identities, as this can play into problematic discourses which position people of colour and queerness as separate. The experience of being expected to choose one identity over another or as more important is troubling for QTPOC. For example, Yuen-Thompson (2012, p. 420) interviewed biracial–bisexual women and found the single-issue focus on sexuality a challenge within the queer community as participants felt that they had to leave their other identities 'at the door'. The women found this fragmentation of lived experience and identity uncomfortable and searched for places in which difference and multiplicity were welcomed. In Chapter 2 I trouble traditional psychological approaches to identity and that a 'cohesive' or unitary identity is possible or even desirable. I argue for a way forward which understands identity and subjectivity as 'always on the way' (Annells, 1996, p. 707).

Giwa and Greensmith (2012, p. 163) note attempts to 'homogenize the different experiences of ethnoracial and cultural groups through the promulgation of a unified community in the symbolic event known as Pride' while LGBTQ people of colour continued to experience pervasive racism. A large amount of research has found that racism in majority white LGBTQ communities in the US harms people of colour and was a 'serious impediment to the participation of people of colour' (Giwa and Greensmith, 2012, p. 172). Kulick et al. (2017, p. 1128) found that many LGBTQ organisations are 'culturally and politically grounded in whiteness, including ... norms grounded in assumptions of white privilege, and acts of implicit and explicit racial bias in these spaces'. They found for students of colour involved in LGBTQ activism on campus that increased visibility of being a LGBTQ person of colour increased the 'stakes of blatant discrimination and harassment', exacerbating their stress (p. 1137).

Hagai, Annechino, Young, and Antin (2020, p. 975) highlight the importance of challenging the universalisation of Western, white LGBTQ narratives of, for example, coming out and in understanding the nuances of coming out for those who are 'low income' and 'BIPOC' (Black, Indigenous, People of Colour). They highlight how 'coming out' intersects with 'multiple jeopardies' of living in a 'culture that privileges whiteness' (p. 975). For example, studies have found that

Black lesbian and bisexual women may come out later and may be less public about their sexual identities as a way of keeping ties with Black communities. As I discuss later this may be due to the lack of discussion around sexuality and sexual behaviour in Black and brown communities who already face pathologisation and being positioned as deviant in relation to white normativity. Similarly, Garvey, Mobley, Summerville, and Moore (2019, p. 170) challenge the idea that 'coming out' is a 'desired and necessary developmental process' for all.

Hagai et al. (2020, p. 980) found that in comparison to white participants fewer 'BIPOC participants positioned sexual identity at the center of their narrated identity'. White ways of emphasising sexual identity did not fit right for BIPOC participants and they felt alienated by the white LGBTQ community. For BIPOC participants their sexual identities were understood as intersecting with their racial and gender identities.

Hagai et al. (2020, p. 987) conclude that activism and re-connecting with community is a part of the 'process of trauma recovery' which is aligned with 'a radical healing perspective that understands healing as grounded in the formation of critical consciousness, hope, and healing communities'. Kulick et al. (2017) argue that activist spaces which centre intersectionality and multiplicity of identity may be more supportive for LGBTQ people of colour. However, Vaccaro and Mena's (2011, p. 340) research highlights the difficulties young QTPOC activists experience including a 'heightened sense of responsibility to others and difficult multiple minority identity explorations which left them experiencing burnout, compassion fatigue, and in some cases suicidal ideation'.

Garvey et al. (2019) trouble queer research which centres whiteness and takes a 'deficit-laden' approach to QTPOC communities. They argue that we must understand structural and institutional inequalities and processes of racialisation, gendering, and sexuality to understand the lived experiences of QTPOC. They encourage an engagement with critical theory – critical race, queer, and intersectional theory – to understand 'pervasive racism and white supremacy in LGBTQ spaces, as well as heterosexist and gendered oppression in spaces of colour' (p. 170).

Pastrana (2010, p. 56) described an 'intersectional imagination' in the experiences of QTPOC he researched; those living with multiple identities and oppressions found it difficult to separate out their experiences from each 'strand' of identity – for them they were all interlinked. The expectation to leave other parts of the self 'at the door' works to overlook the lived complexity of subjectivity and fails to address the ways in which these histories and experiences of oppression interact and may exacerbate feelings of social isolation. Pastrana's (2010) study illustrated how these participants shared a certain angle of vision with other QTPOC holding an analysis of dominant ways of understanding and being from their positions at the intersections of multiple forms of marginalisation. However, a criticism of much of this research is that it focuses on an individual's conceptualisation of multiple identities in isolation from relational, community, social, historical, and cultural contexts.

In the psychological and wider literature, the research points to the problem of the lack of social support for QTPOC. For those experiencing multiple forms of intersecting minoritisation, such as QTPOC, exclusion from multiple traditional support networks because of queer phobia, transphobia, or racism could have a negative impact on wellbeing (Clemon et al., 2012; Millet et al., 2012). Clemon et al. (2012, p. 555) described the experiences of some Black gay men who felt a 'sense of estrangement from black communities' and a 'sense of alienation from all gay communities'.

Jones' (2016) research with a majority white LGBT youth group explored how young people collectively constructed their non-heteronormative identities in opposition to what they positioned as an 'homogenous' homophobic Asian 'other' (p. 119). 'Asians' were conflated with Muslims and constructed as 'illegitimate British citizens' and a 'threat to LGBT equality' (p. 117). The young people utilised the process of 'othering' Asians 'to authenticate their own status as legitimate citizens who should not be marginalised'; creating themselves as an in-group who were LGBT and not-Asian and an out-group who were not-LGBT and Asian (p. 126). This erased the possibility of Asian LGBTQ people and raises issues about how political rhetoric on LGBTQ rights has merged with mainstream British Islamophobia and concerns over the place of Muslims, immigrants, and Black and brown people in the UK – positioning these groups as incompatible with sexual and gender diversity. Jones (2016, p. 127) argues that this reinforces the idea that the 'ideal queer citizen is typically white', erasing the complexity and diversity of Black and brown people's lives. It is interesting to note that one of the participants, Bailey, was mixed race and was recruited into this racist narrative. Bailey's 'own minority ethnic background did not prevent her from producing a group identity and thus positioning herself as a legitimate LGBT citizen; despite being non-white, she was – more importantly – non-Asian' (p. 127). This is troubling itself and raises questions about supporting young QTPOC and the possible consequences this may have for Bailey.

Walker and Longmire-Avital (2013) found in their research that Black LGB people's connections to the Black church and having religious faith was a source of support and wellbeing. It was found that religious faith was significant in contributing to resiliency for these Black LGB people when their own internalised 'homonegativity' was high – this social support was key to their wellbeing (p. 1). However, considering the homonegativity and conservative sexual politics of some Black churches this social support may 'create future vulnerabilities for their psychological wellbeing' (p. 6).

Balsam et al. (2011) found that micro-aggressions experienced by QTPOC are linked to depression and stress, particularly in experiencing racism in LGBT communities, heterosexism in Black and brown communities, and racism in personal relationships. Heterosexism in Black and brown communities was found to be especially harmful to participants. Meyer (2012, p. 853) explored QTPOC experiences of anti-queer violence and found that unlike white queer and trans people, QTPOC had to manage a politics of respectability within their communities of colour, that they had to 'contend with a discourse that they have disappointed their racial communities'. For the QTPOC interviewed, anti-queer violence was interpreted as a punishment for failing to represent their racial communities. The literature then points to the importance of social support for QTPOC and how this is often undermined by the multiple communities they are a part of, failing to support and often openly discriminating against the multiplicity of their experiences.

Queer and Trans People of Colour in the UK: Possibilities for Intersectional Richness seeks to understand how QTPOC activisms may function as a collective way in which QTPOC create shared social support addressing, embracing, and affirming multiplicity while helping to navigate and address racism, queerphobia, and transphobia. I propose QTPOC activisms actively address lack of support from multiple communities and discrimination against and fragmentation of minoritised identities and experience. This addresses the gap in literature on collectivised political action by and for QTPOC, particularly in the UK, and what Akerlund and Cheung (2000, p. 279) called the focus on 'deficits' of QTPOC experience in the literature, by exploring the possibilities of QTPOC activisms.

Pastrana (2010, p. 63) argues that we must look at the oppression experienced by QTPOC, but also 'incorporate how success and resilience is conceived, birthed, nurtured'. This study explored the formation of subjectivity and the intersections of race, gender, and sexuality within the specific British postcolonial context. I examine how QTPOC activist groups create possibilities for intersectional richness – space for collective resistance to the fragmentation of experience, in which to develop a critical consciousness of the intersections of race, gender, and sexuality and to name and resist the intersecting forces of racial, sexual, and gendered oppression in the UK. I highlight the need for an intersectional lens in understanding subjectivity drawing Black feminist, anti-/post-/de-colonial, and queer theory into critical psychology.

Outline of chapters

Queer and Trans People of Colour in the UK: Possibilities for Intersectional Richness has been developed from extensive research as a part of my doctoral study. Chapter 2, Exploring QTPOC Lives, explores the background to the book in more detail – my involvement in QTPOC groups, my training in critical psychology, and how this has shaped my orientation towards the research. I critique traditional psychological approaches to the subject, drawing on anti-/post-/de-colonial, Black feminist, and queer theory to make a critical intervention into critical psychological methodology, epistemology, and ontology disrupting psychology's disciplinary boundaries to make sense of intersectionality, subjectivity, and QTPOC's experiences of being-in-the-world. I discuss the development of a novel 'queerly raced' phenomenological analytic framework drawing on Fanon (1986) and Ahmed's (2006) ground-breaking critiques of phenomenology. I discuss my orientation towards this work, the complexities of writing about the aliveness of being, and the politics and methodology of Black queer feminism and decoloniality against traditional 'objective' and objectifying approaches to psychological inquiry, the role of intersubjectivity, the erotic, and 'feeling one's way' in analysis (Nayak, 2015, p. 33).

Chapter 3, Theorising Multiplicity, addresses the limitations of traditional psychological approaches to race, gender, and sexuality drawing on critical psychology as well as Black feminist, queer, and anti-/post-/de-colonial theory to provide a theoretical framework for the book. This chapter intervenes into psychology challenging the discipline to acknowledge and address the centrality of 'coloniality' and its failure to grasp the importance of addressing whiteness, white supremacy, structural inequalities, and intersectionality in understanding human behaviour, identity, and subjectivities (Quijano, 2007, p. 170).

In Chapter 4, Belonging, I present one of the biggest themes in the book – the question of belonging for QTPOC. I explore the struggle for belonging on the way to finding and creating QTPOC community, how this feels for participants, how they make sense of this process, and the specific British context which troubles and fractures the possibility of belonging. I explore exclusion, the 'white-washing' and fragmentation of the intersectional lived experiences of QTPOC, racial melancholia, and the disorientating processes of racialisation–gendering–sexualisation in post-colonial Britain and the impact on subjectivity.

In Chapter 5, Building Community, building on questions of belonging from Chapter 4 I explore the possibilities provided by QTPOC spaces for connection and affirmation of embodied lived experience; the joy and the erotics of being in community; and as spaces in which to speak back to and resist white hegemony. Drawing on the discussions of racial melancholia from the previous chapter, I consider the potentialities of what Munoz (2007, p. 444) describes as 'feeling together in difference'.

In Chapter 6, Decolonising Gender and Sexuality, I explore how QTPOC spaces supported participants in making sense of coloniality and moving towards decolonising gender and sexuality. This chapter explores this work as well as the development of a critical decolonising consciousness, in which participants grappled with the complex histories of colonisation, immigration, assimilation, and the intersections of race, gender, and sexuality. This shaped the development of their identities and how they understood the tensions around sexual and gender variance within Black and brown communities.

In Chapter 6, Conflict and Harm in Community, I consider some of the issues facing queer activist communities regarding conflict, harm, and abuse and explore some of the issues raised by participants in navigating these issues in QTPOC groups. I draw on current debates and conversations about abolition, transformative justice, and community accountability. I reflect on the significance of the findings discussed in the previous three chapters to centre the potentialities of 'feeling together in difference' and the power of generous and reparative moves towards understanding harm, intersectional trauma, and community.

In Chapter 8, Conclusion, I draw together my analyses and then consider recommendations and implications for future research, practice, and activism. I reflect on the challenge and gift of this book for an intersectional (critical) psychology, academia, and activism.

Notes

1 'Black and brown' is used here against more typical governmental terms such as Black Asian Minority Ethnic (BAME) which continue to be contested. This highlights the difficulties of naming ourselves as a collective of racially minoritised people. Within this book I use different terms depending on who is speaking and who is referenced – terms include 'people of colour', politically Black, and BAME for speaking collectively and specific ethno-racial identifications such as South Asian, Caribbean, Black (of African descent).
2 The inclusion of trans issues within the homonationalist project is questionable as the T in LGBT continues to be marginalised within LGBT movements, and political progress remains frustrated by pervasive cultural and institutional transphobia.
3 For the rest of this book I use 'Black' to mean of African descent.
4 Throughout the book I move between the terms 'people of colour' and 'Black and brown' people, this is dependent on how participants are defined in research cited, as well as how participants in this study name themselves and others. In Chapter 2 I note the slippage of the use of 'people of colour' from a political, coalitional naming towards a naming of individual identity.

2
EXPLORING QTPOC LIVES

This study developed from my background in critical psychology and involvement in community development and organising in QTPOC activist groups. In my work in sexual health prevention, I was disappointed with the ways in which Black and LGBTQ third sector organisations struggled with addressing the intersections of their work, and how Black services were underfunded and seen as unable to address the needs of LGBTQ communities. In my role in a Black third sector organisation I connected with Black queer elders, such as Maria Noble, and radical histories of intersectional organising around HIV, as well as Black lesbian networks that had existed in the 1980s and 1990s. Along the way I met other Black lesbian and queer women – Jessica Creighton, Chloe Cousins, Christina Fonthes, and Zinzi Minnott – who were frustrated by the lack of Black queer community spaces and we decided to create our own. In creating our own space, we challenged the silences and lack of attention to the intersections of race, gender, and sexuality and the idea that we existed in small numbers – there were so many of us, and there was a burgeoning network of QTPOC organisations in development across the UK.

As an activist and critical psychologist, I was perturbed by the silences around queer and trans people of colour – as if Black and brown folks do not have complex subjectivities and rich inner lives, how stereotypes of our perceived deviant and hyper (hetero) sexuality persist and continue to attempt to position us in static, racist ways. I was thrilled by the possibilities of QTPOC spaces and what they meant to those involved, how they might provide possibilities for negotiating the silences, tensions, and difficulties at the intersections of minoritised forms of racialisation, sexuality, and gender and structural forms of racism, queerphobia, and transphobia and how we might make 'liveable' lives together (Browne et al., 2021, p. 32).

As discussed in Chapter 1, much of the previous literature had focused on 'deficit' approaches – the difficulties experienced by QTPOC; however, I was interested in a closer, more nuanced understanding of these complexities. In much of the wider LGBTQ research, Black and brown queer and trans folks were and continue to be positioned as 'hard to reach', as already a problem in their relationship to specific forms and norms of LGBTQ identities, subjectivities, and communities. 'Hard to reach' suggests to 'reach out' of the centre – and in which *the* centre is always, unambiguously but invisibly, normatively white, and Western. The 'coloniality' of knowledge and being – in which *the* 'centre' has become white and Western through 'conquest' – effaces the fact that there were many centres, many knowledges, and ways of being before they collapsed under and into *the* centre (Quijano, 2007, p. 169; Gordon, 2014, pp. 82, 83). What knowledges are there when one decentres the centre, and values knowledge and being that has been minoritised?

This study then comes from *a* centre, of having been embedded within QTPOC networks, of not seeking to 'reach out' from *the* centre but in centring the minoritised communities I was a part of and valuing the knowledges and ways of being within them, questioning how they had been represented in *the* centre, while also being in *the* centre, in the belly of the beast. I was interested in how QTPOC group spaces engendered forms of social and community support to navigate the complexities of multiple, intersecting forms of minoritisation individually and collectively as well as enliven the possibilities of being queer and trans people of colour – as I will discuss later in the book, of joy, the erotics of collectivism, and of reclaiming the intersectional richness of our lives, and their decolonial potentialities. I consider how these collective strengths and riches are utilised to navigate what I interpret as racial melancholia, belonging, and the experience of being 'queerly raced'. I suggest dwelling in these spaces of uncertainty and ambiguity can be productive, 'providing a bridge to connect with multiple others and aspects of self' (Watkins and Shulman, 2008, p. 166). I consider the ways in which QTPOC utilise their experiences of marginality to queer, trouble, and decolonise their own understandings of gender, sexuality, and belonging as well as grapple with questions of addressing harm in community and how this is underlined by and through decolonial love.

In being embedded within these networks, I have struggled with my formal training in psychology and have attempted to resist its objectifying approach and attempts at (white, cis-heteronormative) universality. I have struggled with the ways in which psychology empties the subject, particularly those of us minoritised in myriad ways through coloniality as well as those of us who are majoritised. Psychology desires to pin us in place, like a butterfly in a natural history museum – to claim that we can be known objectively, in our entirety, and fixed in place and time. As a critical psychologist I do not desire to capture the butterfly but to be alongside it, to watch it flutter and soar on the air, the light on its wings, the changing of the seasons, it's aliveness. To understand our beingness in relationship, not as separate but connected. This is a refusal then to pin subjects in place, a critique and rejection of normative ideas of 'fixed', authentic identities; towards an understanding of the 'psychic fragmentation' of coloniality (Watkins and Shulman, 2008, pp. 162, 159; Nayak, 2015). It is an exploration of how queer and trans people of colour might negotiate, disidentify, and challenge multiple intersecting forms of minoritisation and the 'mockeries of separations' that they endure (Lorde, 1977, p. 43 cited in Nayak, 2015). I have focused then on the processes of becoming, of identity and subjectivity as always being 'on the way', of the dynamic production of new forms of subjectivities, and attempting to develop nuanced, complex understandings of race, gender, and sexuality in the formation of queer and trans people of colour's experience of being in the world (Mama, 1995; Annells, 1996, p. 707; Nayak, 2015). This has meant a disruptive approach to psychology, permeating its enforced arbitrary boundaries as a discipline. Psychology is impoverished by its lack of engagement with other forms of thought and attempts to keep itself 'pure' – what Gordon (2014, p. 81) described as 'disciplinary decadence'– with its desire to understand the world only through its own limited frames and definitions, remaining focused on individual and static understandings of the subject at the micro level; in which psychology 'in solipsistic fashion' becomes 'the world' (Gordon, 2014, p. 86). Psychology's disciplinary decadence makes us poorer, reinforcing one specific lens on being – reducing and stifling the complexities, the movement, the nuances of life to behavioural laws, measurable variables, fixed certainties. As Fanon (1952) powerfully argues:

> What is by common consent called the human sciences have their own drama …. All these discoveries, all these inquiries lead only in one direction: to make man admit that he is nothing, absolutely nothing – and that he must put an end to the narcissism on which he relies in order to imagine that he is different from the other "animals." … This amounts to nothing more nor less than man's surrender …. Having reflected on that, I grasp my narcissism with both hands and I turn my back on the degradation of those who would make man a mere [biological] mechanism …. And truly what is to be done is to set man free.
> *(cited in Wynter and McKittrick, 2015, p. 13, emphasis added)*

I refuse this colonial degradation, to empty the subject, to reduce to nothing. Instead, I am motivated by a desire to be alongside, of what it is to be in the world – partial, embodied, 'living' knowledges in the service of the communities I belong to and love, and what it means for subjectivity and the collective to come together (Gordon, 2014, p. 86). In the following chapter I will consider critical theory, such as Black feminist theory, to understand 'the intersecting social and psychic manoeuvres in the process of subject formation', as well as other critical psychological work that troubles notions of fixed, unitary, and fully knowable identities and subjects (Nayak, 2015, p. 21). Nayak (2015, p. 100) argues that in the 'primary task of dismantling borders between race, class, gender, age, sexuality, and (dis)ability, intersectionality performs the solution as the unavailability of a unified solution'. Extending this, I argue that dismantling and disrupting psychology's disciplinary decadence, and disciplinary borders opens us towards the possibilities of the 'unavailability of a unified solution' or a unified *knowing* embracing the potentialities of the partial, the uncertain, the 'in-between', and 'on the way' of knowing and being (Nayak, 2015, pp. 100, 46).

This focus on *being in the world* and being alongside my participants in this study drew me towards phenomenology. Phenomenology emphasises an analysis of self-interpretation, meaning-making, temporality, and intersubjectivity. It stresses the importance of the dialogical encounter with others in understanding oneself and the world around us, as well as situating ourselves within historical, social, and political contexts – challenging the idea of a universal self. This is a focus on being and the process of being and becoming. Phenomenology aims to focus on our 'embeddedness in the world of language and social relationships, and the *inescapable historicity of all understanding*' (Finlay, 2009, p. 11, emphasis added). In comparison to the rational, decontextualised subject of traditional psychology phenomenology supports a critical psychological:

> embrace [of] ambiguity, paradox, descriptive nuance, and a more relational unfolding of meanings ... they recognize the relative, intersubjective, fluid nature of knowledge.
>
> *(Finlay, 2009, p. 15)*

Thinking and interpreting QTPOC experience through a phenomenological analytic framework is helpful to attend to how queer and trans people of colour orient and understand ourselves in the world. I was taken by how a phenomenological analysis could keep me as close as possible to my participants, staying open to both my own and my participants' fluidity, self-interpretation, uncertainty, and the nuances of being-in-the-world – analysis as an intimate dialogical encounter.

However, typical phenomenological methodology in psychology, such as interpretative phenomenological analysis, has drawn on a phenomenology from the *centre*, attending to the 'tactile, vestibular, kinesthetic, and visual character of embodied reality' – of the neutrality or universality of how bodies and subjects are extended in space (Ahmed, 2006, p. 110). This, Fanon (2008, p. 91) notes, ignores the 'historical-racial schema' that underlines which bodies move or are constrained in space, extended, or stopped by the 'skin of the social' (Ahmed, 2006, p. 139). Traditional phenomenology fails to acknowledge how coloniality has made our current world, a world made *white* and shaped the possibilities for being-in-the-world (Ahmed, 2006; Fanon, 2008). Phenomenology has focused on bodies and subjects who are at home in the world, and through the world can extend their reach – bodies and subjects racialised as *white*. Fanon's (2008, p. 90) intervention in phenomenology powerfully disrupts this and centres what it then means to be 'black in relation to the white man' in a world made white.

Black people are 'fixed' in place and time, in which they are 'overdetermined from the outside' through the white gaze and the historical–racial schema (p. 95). Fanon (2008, p. 89) describes entering French society not as a man but as a Black man – not as a subject but as an 'object among other objects'. This is a nauseating, disorientating experience which produces a third-person consciousness where one 'encounters difficulties in elaborating his body schema ... the image of one's body is solely negating' (p. 90). This is an understanding of being-in-the-world through the white gaze, of an 'epidermal racial schema' in which the meaning of your subjectivity is projected onto, into, and through your skin – you do not enter the world as a free subject but 'locked in this suffocating reification' (pp. 92, 89).

Ahmed's (2006) queer phenomenology builds on Fanon's (2008) foundational work attending to the intersection of queerness and racialisation in how we experience and orientate ourselves within the world. Ahmed (2006) explores the experience of disorientation when one fails to be orientated towards *white heteronormativity*, but also the possibilities of this disorientation. Fanon's (1986) analytic approach encourages a turn to the meaning of lived experience and how it is understood and tied to social, economic, historic, and political structures (Desai, 2014). His work emphasises 'an exploration of experience, meaning, embodiment, temporality' in the lives of those experiencing oppression (p. 65). Desai (2014, p. 69) highlights that a Fanonian approach to research encourages 'the adoption of a phenomenological psychopolitical attitude towards the lifeworld', and I would add to this that it must take an *intersectional* approach, taking in the criticisms of Fanon's lack of attention to gender and sexuality.

Drawing on these anti-/post-colonial, Black feminist, and feminist of colour interventions in phenomenology I developed a novel interpretative, intersectional framework – what I called a 'queerly raced' phenomenological framework to explore the messy, sensual, and embodied experience of being-in-the-world for queer and trans people of colour. In this framework I could move between the macro and the micro – moving between coloniality and subjectivity taking a radical approach and centring QTPOC within the post-colonial British context. This framework allowed a close reading of the processes of racialisation–gendering–sexualisation and how participants worked on, with and against these processes and how this shaped their understandings of self, becoming, and subjectivity. In these analyses I drew on Ahmed's concepts of orientation and disorientation; Fanon's third-person consciousness and epidermalisation; and weaved in similar post-colonial, Black feminist, and feminist of colour interventions in psychoanalysis such as Munoz's (1999) disidentification and Eng and Han's (2000) racial melancholia.

Drawing on similar attempts to operationalise phenomenology in psychological research (such as Interpretative Phenomenological Analysis; Smith et al., 2009) in developing my analyses within this phenomenological framework I attended to issues of temporality, spatiality, and intersubjectivity in the ways participants made sense of their experiences within interviews and focus groups. However, in extending this approach into a 'queerly raced' analysis I also attended to any references related to the orientation of 'disorientation', historicity, corporeality, and embodiment in the participants' accounts – this drew explicitly from Fanon and Ahmed's anti-/post-colonial and queer interventions into phenomenology.

This 'queerly raced' phenomenological framework opened the analysis further to an interrogation of the experiences of racialisation–gendering–sexualisation; the social, historical, and political contexts; the body; feeling; meaning-making; and subjectivity. Following Fanon (1986) and Ahmed (2006) this worked as a phenomenological intervention to emphasise the experience of being-in-the-world and the process of becoming for queer and trans people of colour within the specific post-colonial British context.

I described this as a 'queerly raced' phenomenological framework to highlight the inseparability and intersectionality of race, gender, and sexuality, underscoring the centrality of coloniality in understanding being in modernity and that coloniality is foundational to 'post-colonial' struggles of gender and sexuality (Quijano, 2007). It names the queerness of disorientation, third-person consciousness, and intersections of race and gender/sexuality. It holds the queerness of racialisation and the racialisation of queerness, refusing the delinking of cis-heteronormativity and whiteness (Ahmed, 2006).

Following Sedgwick (2003), Munoz (2006, p. 682), and Johnson (2015), the 'queerly raced' phenomenological framework draws together anti-/post-colonial, Black/feminist of colour, and queer theory to make an intervention into phenomenological method as a possibility of understanding embodied intersectionality and being-in-the-world – not as a strong theory which Sedgwick problematised as 'prescriptive and totalising' but as a weak theory. In the pulling together of the different theoretical disciplines I move towards the possibilities of border thinking – 'the stitching together of disciplinary polarizations between psychology and socio-historical accounts' (Johnson, 2015, p. 176). This stitching together, of intersecting theoretical work, welcomes the 'unavailability of a unified solution' (Nayak, 2015, p. 100).

Analysis was driven by this framework, the lived experiences of the participants, and their interpretations of their own experience. Having been involved in these groups in the past I developed a dialogue between myself and the data, interpreting participants' own interpretations of their lived experience. I reflected on my own experiences as I undertook the analysis to acknowledge my own position and my own meaning-making, accepting my own subjectivity, and reflecting on the process of analysis. This could sometimes be confusing, and I would feel overwhelmed with the data; however, I regularly reflected on how I was coding and interpreting the data keeping open to my participants' experiences in conversation with my own, ensuring that I was centring their experiences. This was a difficult but rewarding process. The participants' emphasis on their racialised–gendered–sexualised embodied experiences shaped the analysis, becoming an early step in the development of the 'queerly raced' phenomenological framework.

As a Black, bisexual, and gender plentiful/expansive woman of Black Jamaican and white English and Polish working-class heritage, I came to QTPOC activism for similar and differing reasons to my participants. Therefore, at times I closely identified with some of the themes of the book and this has impacted on my own parallel journey within activist and counselling contexts to make sense of my own place in the world. My participants' feelings of not belonging connected with my own deep sense of not belonging as a function of my race, sexuality, and gender. The politics of intersectionality and disorientation therefore 'struck' me in a personal, academic, and activist capacity; I wrestled with the role of *feeling* in my work fearing over-identifying with participants, or of being accused of being too inward looking. However, I recognise that my personal insight and experience intersecting with practice and critical, rigorous academic thought are of great benefit to this book. Nayak (2015, p. 33, emphasis added) argues that this is a form of Black feminist methodology – the use of the erotic (Lorde, 1984), of being open to others and my own experience, that '*feeling* one's way' is part of the

> dialogical relationship between experience, practice and scholarship [that] produces the methodology of the activism of Black feminist theory, where the how to do, and the doing, of the project intersect.

This is a purposeful refusal to be the objective, objectifying psychologist, centring instead the importance of connection and the recognising of the self in others; 'in contrast to Western measures of validity and reliability, the activism of Black feminist methodology is an erotic process of feeling' (Nayak, 2015, p. 33). This also follows Johnson's (2015, p. 157) writing on Sedgwick's (2003) queer 'reparative ethic', turning towards feeling and critiquing the 'long historical privileging of epistemology over ontology', developing a Black *queer* feminist ontology towards the intersubjective, of feeling, the erotic, love, and the collective. However, a Black feminist practice emphasises the importance of both experience and theory *together,* for conscientisation and as 'tools of critical analysis', cautioning against a reliance on experience alone (Nayak, 2015, p. 67).

This Black queer feminist practice in the book has drawn on my early activist education and organising which came within a politically Black environment where the foundations of anti-racist, affirmative, intersectional solidarity were built. Growing up Black with mixed heritage in a majority white working-class town I felt a deep solidarity with all Black and brown folks – there was only a few of us and we had to back each other up. Even when racism wasn't directed at Blackness, I could feel the heat of it partially directed at me and my Otherness. As Sivanandan (1983) notes, together we were Black in a white world. Despite its shortcomings, this meant the politically Black activist communities in and around the majority Black (of African descent) neighbourhoods I found myself living in and a part of in my twenties were incredibly powerful. These were communities in which we worked together across our recognised differences to fight state violence which touched us all. This politics of solidarity is one which imbues the ways in which I work, live, love, think, theorise, and take action. In this study I have been careful in theorising difference – I am a Black person of mixed heritage, working-class, bisexual, and gender plentiful/expansive woman, therefore I feel a deep solidarity with other queer and trans people of colour. However, I have taken deep care in how I theorise the experiences of those who have different experiences of racialisation, who are trans, who are Muslim, and the myriad differences between us. I hope that this book does justice to these differences, in solidarity.

I am moved in this study through a decolonial impulse to challenge and reject ways of scholarship which dehumanise researcher and researched as if they are separate entities, embracing a 'counter-practice' which values human inter-connection, love, and care between us (Maldonado-Torres, 2016, p. 10). The queerly raced phenomenological framework informed by anti-/post-colonial, Black/feminist of colour, and queer theory and practice helped to attend to embodied intersubjectivity and the dialogical relationship between the person and the world, the 'researcher' and the 'researched' sustained through a politics of solidarity.

This was encouraged by a desire to recognise the aliveness of the research, of the processes of becoming, and attempt to resist the static nature of traditional psychological research. The disruption in orientation to research, as well as methodology and the doing of the research, attended to fluidity, nuance, movement, feeling, inter-connection, and being. However, this desire also competes with the ways in which writing, and the limits of language can flatten and make our lives static, recognising the limits of academic enquiry and the possibilities enlivened through other more creative endeavours such as art and performance to make sense of our being-in-the-world. To address some of these tensions, I utilised photo-elicitation to make space for interview participants creativity in sharing their lived experiences. Two weeks before the interview I asked interview participants to use a digital camera or mobile phone to take photos in relation to the topic 'My experience of being a queer and/or trans person of colour; my experience of QTPOC activism'. At the interview instead of an interview-schedule participants were invited to share and talk about the pictures they had taken. This approach to collecting data provided the opportunity for the exploration of lived experience beyond the spoken word, and for the participants to illustrate and position their own embodied experiences. Photography provided possibilities to explore experiences that are not easily described in 'formal language … [also] formal language can often produce stereotypical and normative representation of feelings, because clients will try to fit their experiences into readily available (and dominant) categories' (Gilles et al., 2005, p. 201).

However, there are continual tensions in the book about how to write about subjectivity and keeping alive the nuance and complexity of subjectivities and identities as always being 'on the way'. In writing about the participants' lived experience there will be a desire for some readers to fix the participants in place, and to universalise their experience, but I hope that my writing encourages readers to stay with 'being' as a process rather than a fixed point. In Chapter 7, I note how some participants were particularly wary of 'QTPOC' being used as a fixed identity, rather than as an umbrella term. It's important that, as discussed in Chapter 1, the term 'queer and trans people of colour' defines queer and trans as umbrella terms and that 'people of colour' is developed from and utilised in a similar way to political Blackness. 'People of colour' is an American term, developed from 'women of colour' which was 'not an ethnicity' but an invention 'of solidarity, an alliance, a political necessity that is not the given name of every female with dark skin and a colonized tongue, but rather a choice about how to resist and with whom' (The Latina Feminist Group, 2001, pp. 102, 103). 'People of colour', like political Blackness, was originally a term for coalition – participants in this study understood the term this way, and participants were drawn from explicitly activist networks who grouped themselves under this coalitional and explicitly political identity. As Ashok/a explained this was 'like a label to put on a room so that you can gather in that room'.

However, the term 'people of colour' was not without its tensions among participants. One older focus group participant, Dorian, described the term as 'weak' and was concerned about other possible reasons that 'Black' had been dropped from the lexicon, implicating the insidious nature of anti-Blackness among wider brown communities. Swaby (2014) has noted a resurgence in the uses of political Blackness as young South Asian feminists have taken this up in recent years as a way of addressing anti-Blackness in their own communities of origin. Other participants saw the term 'people of colour' as an Americanism, with Aflia, a focus group participant, calling it a 'cop out' within the British context and as too dangerously reminiscent of the British, pejorative usage of 'coloured'. However, another focus group participant, Zac, described the term 'people of colour', and its use alongside 'queer' in QTPOC as a 'provocative' statement, as something that 'stands up for itself,' as well as a reclaiming of terms once seen as derogatory. This was in comparison to terms such as Black Asian Minority Ethnic (BAME) that were seen as more bureaucratic, euphemistic, and 'passive'.

Participants did speak of their indebtedness to political Blackness, and as discussed in Chapter 1 the definition of 'people of colour' developed by QTIPOC London was drawn from the definitions of political Blackness from the Black Lesbian and Gay Centre in Peckham, London, in the 1980s. However, 'people of colour' was deemed as more accessible and inclusive to younger people, as well as the changing and more recent Black and brown populations in Britain. The use of the term 'people of colour' was fuelled by a desire to make sure that 'anyone who might half think they belonged knew that they belonged' (Ashok/a), recognising both the limits and critiques of political Blackness.

Participants were concerned by the potential slippage of 'people of colour' from a coalitional term to one of a reified identity. The interviews were undertaken in 2014 and 2015, and these concerns seem to have been prescient. Post-2020 and the murder of George Floyd, institutions and sectors have scrambled for more appropriate ways of naming vastly different populations who are racially minoritised as other – moving away from problematic, governmental terms such as 'Black Asian Minority Ethnic' or 'BAME'. 'People of colour' has begun to circulate as an identity category, detached from its political uses and origins, in which all Black and brown or 'non-white' people can be identified as 'people of colour' – moving from a coalitional grouping to a lumping together. In this book I have used the term 'people of colour' in reference to the QTPOC participants, groups, and networks and used 'Black and brown' to talk of people and communities more widely to note participants' and my own ambivalence about 'people of colour's' depoliticisation and wider usage.

These tensions and uncertainties speak to the difficulties of naming ourselves and our experiences, our differences – grappling with categorisations borne of coloniality, of 'race', 'gender', and 'sexuality' in some forms challenged and reclaimed as well as troubled. There are tensions around these categories as constraining and as reifying coloniality, while also powerfully, politically, and collectively naming our experiences in the world and the processes through which we are racialised, gendered, sexed and how this is navigated, negotiated, and shapes our subjectivities. Additionally, the limits of language mean that writing about intersectionality can flatten the richness of our experiences, and the complexities. In this work I move between the grouping of 'QTPOC' as a political and group identification and the specificities of, for example, Black folks and the intersections of race, sexuality, and gender – but even this collapses the diversity of experience into one that is more broadly 'Black British'. Participants in this study identified with their own specific experiences such as Ashok/a, who identified as a 'Working Class, Brown, South Asian/Bengali, Bi, Queer, Trans, Genderfucker', as well as placing themselves alongside others with similar and differing experiences under the umbrella of QTPOC. As the author I have had to make broad strokes of understanding complex and contested categories, their reclamation, and processes of racialisation, gender, sexuality that shape subject formation. This work is part of the process of attempting to hold these myriad complexities – how people come together to make sense of being-in-the-world and the complexities of structural and embodied intersectionality, of those who have come together in a room they have labelled 'QTPOC'.

Conclusion

In this chapter I have reflected on the background to this study, my involvement in QTPOC activist groups, and my training in critical psychology. I have been critical of traditional objective and objectifying approaches to research which seek to fix subjects in place, and instead aimed to centre an understanding of being as 'always on the way', centring intersubjectivity, fluidity, uncertainty, and the development of new forms of subjectivity and identity (Annells, 1996, p. 707). Drawing on Gordon's (2014) critique of 'disciplinary decadence', I have sought to disrupt psychology's disciplinary boundaries, drawing on anti-/post-colonial,

Black feminist, and queer theory to understand 'the intersecting social and psychic manoeuvres in the process of subject formation' (Nayak, 2015, p. 21). In Chapter 3 I explore this further, explicating critical psychological work that has disrupted these understandings of the subject, as well as exploring other critical theories outside of psychology and those marginalised in psychology, particularly around race and coloniality – drawing them in to disrupt psychology and move towards an intersectional understanding of subjectivity and being.

This disruptive impulse has shaped both the content and the form of the research, following Nayak (2015, p. 33) there is a 'dialogical relationship between experience, practice and scholarship', which Nayak describes as the 'methodology of the activism of Black feminist theory, where the how to do, and the doing, of the project intersect'. The dialogical relationship between experience, practice, and scholarship has informed my epistemological and ontological orientation drawing my methodological stance towards a disruption in phenomenology to develop a queerly raced analytic framework shaped by a Black queer feminist methodology which welcomes the role of the erotic process of 'feeling one's way'.

I hope the focus on feeling, intersubjectivity, of being as 'always on the way' keeps a sense of aliveness to my writing and the understanding of subjectivity and being. I have noted the limitations of the written form and academic enquiry in flattening the richness of our lives and their complexities, nuances, fluidity; how this is also shaped by the difficulties of naming ourselves as minoritised people and attending to categories of being borne of coloniality. I am excited by the 'unavailability of a unified solution', of the possibilities of openness to the partiality of knowledge, of nuance and uncertainty for knowing and being – as a 'counter-practice' to the coloniality of fixed and universal knowledges and ways of being (Watkins and Shulman, 2008; Nayak, 2015, p. 100; Maldonado-Torres, 2016, p. 10).

3
THEORISING MULTIPLICITY

Introduction

At the beginning of my doctoral study, I was frustrated by the lack of theory and analytical frameworks within psychology that could engage with the multiplicity of experience of my queer and/or trans people of colour participants. There was little that could address intersectionality and the interlocking nature of systems of power such as white supremacy, colonialism, patriarchy, and heteronormativity. In this chapter I critique the limitations of traditional and critical psychology; their engagements with understanding sexuality, gender, and race; illuminate marginalised work in these areas; and challenge the paucity of work in the psychology mainstream to understand intersectional lived experience. I then chart the development of my own framework for this book – drawing on critical psychology and offering a critical intervention into both psychology and critical psychology. In this intervention I consider the psychosocial turn, drawing on post-colonial and Black feminist theory alongside minoritised voices in psychology such as Fanon to develop a framework for understanding intersectional subjectivities and the lived experiences of queer and trans people of colour. Following Chapter 2, this chapter presents a turn to embodiment, materiality, and affect to explore the messy, sensual lived experience of being-in-the-world, in particular following Fanon (1986), for those who live at the intersections of minoritised race, gender, and sexuality, examining what Nayak (2015, p. 91) described as the difficulties of 'embodied intersectionality'.

The limitations of traditional psychology and development of critical psychology

Critical psychology has questioned the ways psychology has tended to work in the service of the status quo, pointing out 'the epistemological, ethical and political shortcomings of psychology, and how it serves the interests of powerful groups' (Teo, 1999, p. 122; Parker, 2015). Psychology has been critiqued for its attempts to elevate itself as part of the natural sciences using positivist methods which reductively emphasise the individual in isolation from the social (Fanon, 1986; Wynter and McKittrick, 2015). In this approach to human experience researchers attempt to disconnect themselves from their participants, creating a hierarchical power dynamic in the name of 'objectivity' or 'neutrality' (Parker, 2015, p. 4). This often leads to a failure to recognise social, historical, economic, and political contexts and a tendency to ignore issues of power and structural inequalities. The subject of psychology has been traditionally defined as 'unitary, rational', helping to 'constitute the very form of modern individuality' and how we understand ourselves (Henriques et al., 1984, p. 1). Cognitive and behaviourist approaches have been favoured within the discipline, encouraging research which will find laws, rules, and prescriptions for understanding human behaviour. As a 'science' psychology staunchly positions itself as separate from the political, and therefore questions of social justice and equality. Structural forms of power such as patriarchy, white supremacy, and capitalism are understood as the analytic domain of sociology and therefore irrelevant to the psychological study of the individual.

Critical psychology has drawn on critical theory, philosophy, cultural theory, feminism, and post-colonialism to challenge traditional psychological approaches to the subject. These critical engagements precipitated and unfolded from the oft-discussed 'crisis' in social psychology in the 1960s, borne of the frustration and discontent with traditional social psychological approaches. Social psychology was criticised for being, at times, 'artificial', 'trivial', 'fragmented', 'reductionistic', 'conceptually and theoretically naïve', 'narrowly focused on individualism', and 'irrelevant for understanding social issues and problems' (Kim, 1999, p. 2). Critiques came from both within and outside of the field and coincided with a wave of political unrest and social change in the West in the forms of Civil Rights and Black Power, feminist movements, and gay liberation alongside the struggles for independence in (formerly) colonised countries in the Global South (Gough, 2015). The forms of experiential and theoretical knowledge emerging from these liberation struggles troubled the universalism of psychology, its role as a 'disciplining institutional force', and the ways in which certain subjects were positioned as problems, for example, Black and brown people, women, LGBT people, those with mental health problems and their intersections (p. 108). At the same time critiques and experimental approaches from 'human potential pioneers' such as Maslow, as well as a turn to the work of European philosophers such as Heidegger 'led to the development of humanistic, experiential and phenomenological forms of qualitative research' (p. 108). These events inspired a proliferation of critical psychological work, for example, the emergence of feminist psychology, as well as the development of social constructionism and the turn to language, representation, and embodiment in psychology to explore subjectivity.

The turn to language and the emergence of social constructionist approaches challenged psychologists to 'extend … enquiries beyond the individual into social, political and economic realms', understanding knowledge as 'historically and culturally specific' (Burr, 1999, p. 13). This coincided with anti-colonial struggle and the collapse of Empire, challenging hegemonic Western epistemology. Burr (1999, p. 5) broadly described social constructionist assumptions as including a critical approach to the taken-for-granted; that knowledge is historically and culturally situated; that knowledge is constructed through 'social interaction' particularly through language; and social constructions of the world are 'bound up with power relations'.

Social constructionism argues that language is a form of social action, with 'consequences, restrictions and obligations' tied to what we say (p. 8). Social constructionist approaches have drawn on the deconstruction work of poststructuralist philosophers such as Michel Foucault and Jacques Derrida which is 'concerned with how the human subject becomes constructed through the structures of language and through ideology' (p. 17). Power, discourse, and ideology shape the subject, and to paraphrase Derrida, to analyse the formation of subjectivity 'there is nothing beyond the text'. He suggests that it is through critically interrogating the use of language and discourse we may understand the subject.

Engagement with deconstruction theory in critical psychology has produced Foucauldian Discourse Analysis (FDA) which works to interrogate 'prevailing societal discourses and their effects, particularly on marginalized groups' (Gough, 2015, p. 108). FDA focuses on the 'reproduction, reworking and resistance to salient societal discourses' (p. 110). A discourse is a set of 'meanings, metaphors, representations, images, stories, statements and so on' that present social phenomena, events, and people in a certain way (Burr, 1999, p. 64). The emphasis is on the ways in which phenomena are represented in discourse, and a discourse analysis troubles what are described as common-sense or taken-for-granted assumptions.

These developments in critical psychology have aimed to challenge how the subject is understood within psychology, critiquing the idea of a rational, unitary subject, and deconstructing this as a historically situated and socially constructed ideal. The turn to language, deconstruction, and social constructionism provides an alternative – situating the subject within discourse, power, and ideology. However, for some the turn to language and the idea that 'there is nothing beyond the text' leads to an 'impoverished subject', failing to address the complexity of subjectivity and the embodied experience of being-in-the-world (Gough, 2015, p. 110). This conception of the subject is seen as too passive and over-determining – the subject is shaped by discourse, but there is more to subjectivity than discourse (Blackman et al., 2008). This fails 'to recognise that there is more to subjectivity, an excess which pertains to forms of social imagination which are beyond existing representations, which are affective, contentious and not yet realized' (Papadopoulos, 2008, p. 148).

A constructivist approach does not make room for understanding something which is not yet represented in discourse, or how new political subjectivities are formed, for example, political Blackness and QTPOC. This calls for a more nuanced understanding of the workings of power – as that which forms and constrains the subject, while also something the subject resists and works upon in relation to other subjects. Tischner (2013, p. 35) argues that this means that 'while the availability of certain discourses produces particular possibilities of "doing" and "being", subjectivities are not only imposed and either accepted or rejected, but produced and reproduced through embodied experiences within these fields of possibilities'. This conceptualisation of subjectivities allows us to comprehend

> how subjectivities construct new materialities … how subjectivities materialize in new cultural relations and relations of intimacy … how, finally subjectivities contribute to the emergence of new political engagements and new social movements.
> *(Mama, 1995; Blackman et al., 2008, p. 16)*

Additionally, a focus on the 'subjectifying force of language' alone has led to a lack of engagement in critical psychology with the messy, 'bodily, sensuous' experiences of the subject (Blackman, 2002, pp. 134, 135). Blackman (2002, p. 135) points out how discursive approaches may attempt to challenge the rational subject; however, they work to reinforce this notion – of the subject as a rational 'discourse user' (p. 135).

Similarly, Brown and Stenner (2009, p. 90) draw on the work of Antonin Artaud to make similar critiques of discursive psychology; that language and text fail to capture our full lived experience. Artaud argued that

> writing [or text] is pigshit when it reduces the movement of thought (aka "the obscure", "the unknown") to the empty abstraction of humanism, i.e. the self-contained, self-possessive model of the person whose mind is dominated by the faux-drama of petit bourgeois mortality and intimacy.
> *(Brown and Stenner, 2009, p. 92)*

Brown and Stenner (2009) are arguing against the poverty of traditional psychological research, as well as the purely critical discursive approach as incapable of addressing the chaotic, embodied experience of being human. It can be argued that discursive approaches are still tied to Cartesian dualism which remains foundational to Western thought; that is, the ontological idea that 'to experience oneself as a "thinking thing" is then to experience oneself as immaterial, as divorced from a dubious and untrustworthy body' (p. 94). Brown and Stenner (2009) highlight the limitations of focusing on language and text in psychology and encourage a turn towards embodiment and affect.

Feminist psychoanalysis has provided possibilities for attending to embodiment. Helene Cixous argued that women are 'excluded from Western philosophy and culture'; and through this exclusion women have been 'allocated everything that men deny about themselves' (Craib, 2001, p. 172). As previously discussed, the anti-/post-colonial work of Fanon (2007) has criticised Western philosophy for excluding Black and brown people and the formerly colonised in its conceptions of the world and the 'universality' of, for example, Freud and Sartre's work. Fanon (2007) chronicles the psychodynamic dialectic between white and Black, in which the repressed and denied fantasies of the white man are projected onto the bodies of the colonised.

The decolonial work of Quijano (2007) describes European 'modernity/rationality', within which psychology is rooted, as a form of coloniality, and as such the 'most general form of domination in the world today' (pp. 170, 171). The classification of humans via the constructs of race, gender, and sexuality emerged during colonialism through which Europeans established their own biological, structural, and cultural superiority and their own epistemology as the 'universal paradigm of knowledge' (p. 172). Within this paradigm male Europeans are defined as rational subjects vis-à-vis the objectified Other or objectified nature. Decolonial critiques have thus challenged modernity/rationality as a distinctly geographic and historically located power–knowledge matrix, disputing its claim of universality. These have contested the foundations of European thought, and of traditional psychology's rational subject as well as allowing the objectified Other to speak and be heard. Drawing on these forms of critical theory, critical psychologists have sought to complicate the relationship between self and society, psyche and culture challenging the dualism of traditional psychology and disputing the boundaries between interior and exterior worlds. These have worked to contradict the 'atomistic image of social existence in general' (Quijano, 2007, p. 173).

Feminist psychoanalysis and Fanon's (2007, p. 2) anti-/post-colonial writings provide glimpses into the experience of alterity, the 'zone of non-being' for the formerly colonised, and of being excluded from official histories. Kristeva (1980, p. 166) considers the women's struggle as 'introducing ruptures, blank spaces and holes into language', addressing the registers of embodied lived experience that have 'not been grasped by the linguistic or ideological system'. Fanon (2007, p. 4) utilises phenomenological and psychoanalytic inquiry to explore the embodied experience of exclusion – the 'internalization – or, better epidermalization' of Black inferiority. This work challenges the power of language; the classification of the human and of difference; and traditional ideas of the subject within Western epistemology and ontology while also attending to embodied experiences of alterity.

Hook (2008, p. 475) is critical of a lack of real engagement with post-colonial work, such as that of Fanon (2007) in critical psychology, noting that it is 'conspicuous' in its absence particularly as much post-colonial theory is 'explicitly psychological in both its concerns and critical resources'. Post-colonial theory provides ways of thinking through 'the psychological and the political, the affective and the structural, the psychical and the governmental', fitting perfectly with critical psychology's own aims and the need to extend these to intersectional embodied racialised, sexualised, and gendered experience (p. 476).

Heeding some of these criticisms, Burr (1999) and Ussher (2008, p. 1782) call for a critical psychological engagement in corporeality particularly for research on gender, sexuality, and race which are experienced at the level of the body, suggesting an approach in which the 'materiality' of the body is always understood as 'mediated by culture, language, and politics'.

Critical psychology troubles traditional approaches to the subject and its engagements with race, gender, and sexuality. However, I concur with Hook (2008) that it could be further engaged with decolonial and post-colonial theory on the particularities of racialisation, subjectification, and embodiment and the intersections with gender and sexuality – and that which is particularly lacking within the British context. In the next part of this chapter, I look to critical psychological research in the areas of gender, race, and sexuality and argue for an approach rooted in intersectionality and a Fanon-inspired anti-/post-/de-colonial framework to ground research into queer and trans people of colour in the UK.

Orientations to race, gender, and sexuality in psychology and critical psychology

Critical psychological work has explored the subjugation and subjectification of those classified as inferior and Other within Western society and through Western philosophy and science. Traditional psychology can be understood as a disciplining force, complicit in the oppression of women, Black and brown people, LGBTQ people, and in the maintenance of the status quo. This has included the use of evolutionary theory to explain male dominance and women's subjugation such as attempts to normalise sexual violence against women (see the development of Coercive Paraphilic Disorder by Vernon L. Quinsey, 2010[1]); the use of typically white, middle-class, Western cisgender, heterosexual men in research who are assumed to be the 'norm' against which others are compared and often classified as abnormal; and the use of essentialist arguments to define 'sex differences' in cognitive, developmental, psychoanalytic, and neuro-psychology (Capdevila and Lazard, 2015, p. 191). Tosh (2015, p. xi, 115) suggests psychology's 'prurient' interest in sexuality and gender identity could be considered 'perverse', and its conceptualisation of gender diversity as well as sexual violence 'deviant' and 'abnormal'. Instead of listening to those minoritised through patriarchal and cis-normative violence psychology 'clings to biomedical discourse, neglecting to consider context and intersecting issues', maintaining the status quo and the oppression of women, children, and trans people (p. 115).

Early traditional psychological and sexological work continues to shape contemporaneous approaches to the study of sexual orientation, of which 'homosexuality' and its 'causes' remain a central focus. Johnson (2015, p. 22) critiques the proliferation of biological research into homosexuality as pathologising, noting that despite changes in the law to legalise homosexuality in the mid-twentieth century, this research as well as the public's interest in it continues to position it as disorder and 'developmentally inferior' (see the continued search for biological markers for sexual behaviours and identities such as finger length ratios, for example, Watts, T.M., Holmes, L., Raines, J., Orbell, S., & Rieger, G. (2018)[2]). Similarly, psychology's refusal to engage with structural inequalities or acknowledge historical and social contexts means that it continues to 'privilege cognitive factors' to understand racism (Henriques et al., 1984, p. 59; Riggs and Augoustinos, 2005). Traditional approaches suggest, for example, that racism is due to individual attitudes or the typical ways in which normative human cognition works rather than an issue of structural inequity and harm. Henriques et al. (1984, p. 58) point out the 'compatibility of social psychology's concept of racial prejudice with existing power relations and its implications for social psychology's reproduction of these social relations'. These approaches naturalise 'race' as an ahistorical, universal form of difference, occluding the social construction of the concept during colonisation and enslavement. They position racism as a natural outcome of human cognitive error, racism as an attitude rather than a structure – emphasising individual over social context and as a simple in-group and out-group dynamic, a liberal understanding of difference as 'skin colour' rather than a historical, social, and political construction of inferiority and (white) supremacy. Traditional psychological approaches to understanding racism collude with white supremacy to occlude structural racism as foundational to the modern Western world, positioning it instead as an 'aberrant ideological affront to the enduring ideals of Enlightenment' which works to continue 'the sense of an exemplary and regulatory western civilisation' (Hesse, 2004, p. 22).

Critical psychology has therefore engaged with feminist, queer, and to a lesser extent post-colonial critiques, with each providing scrutiny of the relationships between psychology's positivist orientation, basis in Western epistemology and ontology, and these different forms of subjugation. Feminists and post-colonial theorists have criticised the individualistic focus of psychology, and the separation of the individual from the wider social, political, and historical contexts (Henriques et al., 1984; Mattos, 2015). Critical psychologists have used the work of Foucault and queer theory to interrogate how psychology has been involved in the construction of modern understandings of sexuality. Foucault's genealogical approach has been utilised to challenge the common-sense assumption that we have moved from the sexually repressive 'dark ages' of the Victorian times towards an ever-increasing liberal progressiveness. Foucault argued that the psy-disciplines have in fact shaped the 'technology of sex' which has created sex as a concern for a secular society and a 'concern of the state and all the individuals within it' (Alldred and Fox, 2015, p. 203). Alldred and Fox (2015, p. 203) follow that psychology and its theories of sex and sexuality have increased the 'surveillance and disciplining' of our intimate lives. They point to psychology and the psy-disciplines as complicit in the construction of an individualistic model of sexuality which has shaped 'Western understandings of what sexuality is, and the limits of what may be thought "sexual"' (p. 203).

Critical psychology then seeks to deconstruct the positivist claims to the 'truth' of human sexuality and illuminate how this research is 'itself productive of how sexualities are understood more widely by people and by social organisations and by institutions' (p. 203). Queer theory has situated modern constructions of sexuality and sexual orientation as forms of 'contemporary capitalist biopolitical action, where discourses and modern technologies about sex and identities participate in controlling life' (Penaloza and Uback, 2015, p. 341). Similarly, Henriques et al. (1984) are critical of social and cognitive psychology's individualistic focus on racism and prejudice as simply an aberration of individual rationality and logic obscuring the history of 'race' as a social and political construct. This erases how racist ideologies and the processes of racialisation have been embedded within Western social structures through colonialism and enslavement, shaping modern race relations (Golash-Boza, 2016).

Critical engagements in this area therefore encourage a challenge to the positivism of traditional psychology and a change in paradigm to address the lived experience of those marginalised through race, gender, and sexuality and their intersections. A critical approach must emphasise an attention to the historical and social construction of knowledge and how this is bound up in power.

Feminist, queer/LGBTQ, and post-colonial theory have provided a way for critical psychology to develop forms of analysing the subject as formed within wider heteronormative, patriarchal, white supremacist and post-colonial structures. Feminist psychology developed a robust critique of traditional psychology's positivism, objectivity, and empiricism. Feminist academics, such as Donna Haraway (1988), troubled the idea of objectivity by illuminating the 'radical historical specificity' and 'contestability' of scientific claims (p. 578). She used the metaphor of vision to critique the limits of objectivity, by insisting on 'the embodied nature of all vision and so reclaim the sensory system that has been used to signify a leap out of the marked body and into the conquering gaze from nowhere' (p. 581). She highlights the power of the gaze of the 'un-marked positions of Man and White', working to mark them as specific, embodied, and subjective (p. 581). Rejecting the dynamic of the un-marked position marking the bodies of the colonised, racialised, gendered, sexualised, she called for a 'doctrine of embodied objectivity' or 'simply situated knowledges' (p. 581). She argued for a feminist science centring the 'politics and epistemologies of location, positioning, and situating' and which recognises the 'partiality' of knowledge, resisting claims to universal knowledge (p. 589).

Haraway's 'situated knowledges' was an attempt to attend to lived experience and knowledge creating a 'feminist critical empiricism' (p. 581). Haraway (1988) struggled with and against the radical constructivism of poststructuralist critiques of science, which in their extreme pointed towards relativism, potentially undermining aims for social change. Similarly, to the history of critical psychology I charted earlier, Haraway (1988) and other feminist academics have engaged with deconstructionism but have also sought to understand embodied and material experience beyond text – the so-called 'extra-discursive' (Burr, 1999, p. 196). Feminist psychology challenges the ways psychology defines the normative, revealing what is defined as objectivity in psychology as a transparent, oft-disembodied male, white subjectivity. It questions how traditional psychological epistemologies '(re)produce hierarchies and sexism in psychological knowledge and practices' (Matto, 2015, p. 335). Feminist psychology has had a significant impact in the development of critical psychology.

Within the field of sexuality, Johnson (2015, pp. 1/2) suggests a third critical possibility to the current 'polarization' between the psychic and the social, in which the psychic focuses on the internal, individual processes of sexuality such as the psychodynamic and biology, and the social points 'to the social field as the defining force that shapes the meanings given to sexuality and sexual experience'. She suggests a turn to the psychosocial and seeks to 'stitch and mend the polarization', bringing together historical and social situatedness with affect, neuroscience, and psychoanalysis to rethink sexual subjectivity (p. 2). This is a potential path out of the problems associated with the binary of essentialism vs social constructionism and the question of what is beyond the text.

Johnson (2015) troubles the critical turn towards text and discourse alone calling for a critical re-engagement with the embodied-ness of sex, sexual orientation, and sexuality. Johnson draws on Sedgwick's (2003) queer 'reparative ethic' in which there is a turn towards feeling which critiques the 'long historical privileging of epistemology over ontology' (Johnson, 2015, p. 157). This is a turn towards intersubjectivity, feeling, 'community and experience rather than language, culture and knowing' (p. 157). Johnson champions a psychosocial approach to sexualities which also seeks to 'reimagine the psychological' through transdisciplinary work, drawing on psychology, sociology, and queer theory among others to go beyond the polarisation between psychological and 'socio-historical' understandings of sexuality (p. 176).

Radical Black psychology also provides a rich alternative to traditional approaches to race and racism. Fanon (1986, p. 14) undertook a psycho-analytic, phenomenological study of his own and others' experiences of colonialism: how the 'juxtaposition of the white and Black races has created a massive psycho-existential complex'. He forcefully described the 'inferiority complex' created by the 'death and burial' of pre-colonial cultures by European colonisers, and the crisis in self-identity he found in himself when he met the 'white man's eyes' (p. 111). It is through contact with the white world that Fanon (1986) comes to the realisation that he does not have access to the universality of 'liberté, egalité, fraternité' of his French colonial 'brothers'; that he was not a man in the same sense, but was a *Black* man, a n★gger – and that the associated stereotypes preceded him. He comes to the crushing realisation that it 'is not I who make a meaning for myself, but it is the meaning that was already there, pre-existing, waiting for me' (p. 134). Fanon (1986) experiences this at the level of the body, the skin – these ideas about Blackness form a 'definitive structuring of the self' (p. 111). Fanon's (1986) work emphasises the phenomenological experience of being racially oppressed, at the affective and bodily level, painting a picture of the colonised's experience of 'being-in-the-world'. He argues that there is a Manichean dynamic between coloniser and colonised, white and Black in which the base, bodily, and fecund are projected onto the racialised other. Whiteness becomes associated with rationality, thinking, logic while Blackness is associated with sensuality, nature, sin, and evil and the Black person desires after whiteness. This symbolism is not simply 'imposed' on the colonised, Fanon (1986, p. 111) argues, but is a 'definitive structuring of the self and the world – definitive because it creates a real dialectic between my body and the world'.

Hook (2008, p. 2) is critical of the lack of research into embodiment and race and the 'neglect' of the work of the South African psychologist Chabani Manganyi (1973, 1977, 1981 cited in Hook, 2008) by social psychology. Manganyi explored the 'psycho-existential crisis of embodiment' (p. 3). For Manganyi, from a psychoanalytic perspective, the body was not just a problem of 'ego-denial (as in the disavowal of the crass physicality of its wastes and wants)', nor is it a problem of 'alienating depersonalization', but that embodiment creates the 'existential dilemma of the disharmonious body-to-ego relationship' (pp. 3/4). According to Manganyi this existential dilemma 'arises' from the contradiction between our own mortality and limitations as bodies and the never-ending possibilities of human consciousness (p. 4). Manganyi suggests that 'ideological symbolization…provides some relief from this pressing existential anxiety of the body' (p. 5). Like Fanon, Manganyi 'insists' that the 'most persistent and categorical of the available symbolic equations in Western culture … is that which equates *whiteness* with *mind* and *Blackness* with the *bodily*' (p. 7). Manganyi argues that it is through this dynamic that the colonised and coloniser, the white and the Black, find identification with whiteness as a 'narcissistic self-valorization … symbolic idealization' and Blackness as 'devalued, deserving of denial and repression' (p. 7).

Manganyi understands the process of racialisation as having a 'phenomenological dimension', supporting Fanon's (1986) attention to the 'sensuality' of race and racism experienced at the 'embodied, affective and experiential level' (Hook, 2008, p. 15, p). Hook (2008, p. 13) notes the emphasis on the physical–psychological experience of being 'surrounded by the presence, the metaphysics of whiteness' in Fanon (1986) and Manganyi's work. Similar to other debates in critical psychology, Hook (2008, p. 15) illuminates the discursive and what he describes as the 'pre-discursive' forms of racism. He makes a distinction between two ways of understanding the racialised body, as the body that can 'both be over-determined by symbolic and ideological means (via various structural impositions) and yet also function, in its capacity as "surface of experience" (affectivity, visceral reactions)' (p. 16). These two ways of understanding the racialised body are troubled by their 'constitutive irresolvability', the tension between the two and the impossibility of knitting the two together (p. 16). However, both must be considered together in work on embodiment and race, as well as subjectivity and the phenomenological experience of 'being-in-the-world'.

This rich critical work into race, gender, and sexuality provides valuable theoretical background in taking a critical psychological approach to queer and trans people of colour's lived, embodied experience. However, the possibility of knitting together the discursive and embodied, material subjectivity is frustrated by understanding race, gender, and sexuality as separate. Race, gender, and sexuality are intersecting, just as white supremacy, patriarchy, and heteronormativity are interlocking and co-constructive.

Academics such as Mama (1995), Lewis (2000), Phoenix (2013, p. 102), and Nayak (2015) have explored '(post) colonial legacies', and the intersections of race and gender and the formation of subjectivity. Phoenix (2013, p. 103) illustrates in her work with Black women in education in the UK that they do not passively take on specific social identities but

> continually develop new consciousness through personal struggles with the contradictions and subjugation they face. Their subjectivities are, therefore, part of a continuous, creative and dynamic process.

Phoenix (2013) illustrates how her participants struggle with and against colonised representations and racist discourses about themselves. Mama (1995, p. 111) encourages us to consider racism as 'texturing subjectivity' but cautions against over-determining racism in Black life. She illuminates the processes through which Black British women involved in the Black feminist movements of the 1980s and 1990s 'collectively' and individually negotiated racist discourses (p. 112). Her participants had to come to terms with being Black in a 'white-dominated milieu', while often being denied their Britishness (p. 116). Similarly, to other work discussed in this chapter, Mama (1995) conceptualises 'subjective processes' as 'being at once socio-historical and intra-psychic' (p. 164). Mama's (1995, p. 89) work 'enables us to transcend the dualism which has so far separated the individual and the social in psychological and social theory'.

Nayak (2015, p. 51) draws Black feminist theory and the work of Audre Lorde into critical psychology to explore how 'racist social structures create racist psychic structures' and how this 'operates differently for Black and white people'. She argues that Black and white people are 'interpellated differently' within racist social structures and that power forms our subjectivity (p. 63). Following Butler, Nayak (2015) blurs the distinction between the internal and external, arguing that it is the process of internalisation of inferiority which creates the distinction (of internal and external) in the first place. It is the emphasis on social context which is important to draw from critical psychology; however, Nayak (2015, p. 21) utilises Black feminist theory to help us to understand the '*intersecting* social and psychic manoeuvres in the process of subject formation' and the 'psychological impact of racism and sexism'. This theoretical work allows for a nuanced understanding of the workings of power in subject formation, making space for the ways in which subjects are positioned within discourses and how they respond to, reproduce, resist, and work on power. This moves us away from the fixed, static notion of essentialist identities, or the subject as over-determined within discourse as in constructivist accounts to an understanding of subjectivity as always on the way, partial, not fully knowable, and in flux. This forces us to balance our understanding of power – that the subject is not over-determined by discourse and that power is decentralised.

The theory of intersectionality troubles the fragmentary impulses of psychology and critical psychology, as it 'challenges mutually exclusive categories of experience and analysis', calling attention to the intersections of race, gender, and sexuality (p. 16). This rejects the traditional subject of psychology as rational and unitary with a 'fixed, stable, totalized identity' (p. 90). Black feminist theory is borne out of the 'interaction of theory with lived experience', a praxis-orientated critical theory which contrasts with traditional psychological methods of objectivity and positivism (p. 32). Nayak (2015, p. 91) considers the potential of Lorde's work on difference compared to psychology's emphasis on the universal; Lorde's work focused on

> the tribulations of relating across difference and transgressing externally imposed ideological, structural, emotional and psychic borders used to separate, distort, and fragment.

This is of key importance to critical psychology – to address fragmentation of the subject and address intersectionality.

In the next section I consider intersectionality alongside Fanon's anti-/post-/de-colonial theory in making sense of the links between race, gender, and sexuality as forms of classification, suggesting how critical psychology and the current examination of queer and trans people of colour lives will be enriched by this, particularly within the UK context.

Intersectionality: threading race, gender, and sexuality together in critical psychology

'Intersectionality' was borne out of the theorisation of women of colour's lived experience by Black and women of colour activists and academics within a long continuum of Black and women of colour feminist work. Intersectionality understands structural forms of oppression – white supremacy, patriarchy, heteronormativity, and capitalism – as interlocking and co-constitutive. Black feminists and feminists of colour argue therefore that race, gender, and sexuality co-construct one another. Intersectionality offers a critique of psychology in that we need to address the macro domains of power – the structural, cultural, and disciplinary and how they intersect in order to understand the micro conditions of our lives at the interpersonal level and the formation of subjectivity (Hill Collins and Bilge, 2020). At the 'interpersonal' level intersectionality challenges the idea of universal, fixed categories of identity and experience and calls attention to the ways in which race and gender and sexuality (among other vectors) intersect with and co-construct one another (Hill Collins and Bilge, 2020, p. 6).

Black feminists and feminists of colour have critiqued the universal category of 'woman' and a feminism that treated 'race and gender as mutually exclusive categories of experience and analysis', arguing that single-axis analyses of gender or race or sexuality leave groups such as Black women, and more recently queer and trans people of colour, 'theoretically erased' (Crenshaw, 1989, p. 40). Working from a critical legal studies framework, Kimberle Crenshaw critiqued the single-axis analysis found in anti-discrimination law as it misrepresented the complexity of Black women's experiences by occluding gendered racialisation. In her analysis of discrimination lawsuits Black women were failed by a legal system which defined discrimination along a single axis – as either gender or racial discrimination. In a case study, Crenshaw found that Black women who sued for gender discrimination in employment opportunities at General Motors lost their case as it was found that the company had employed women – however these were white women. The courts refused to believe that Black women required an understanding of discrimination specific to their experiences as women racialised as Black. In another case, Black women won a racial discrimination case; however, the specificity of their experiences was seen as too different to the experiences of Black men within the company, and therefore the Black men did not receive the compensation the women received. Crenshaw (1989, p. 63) describes these cases as contradictory; however, this stems from the 'conceptual limitations of the single issue analyses that intersectionality challenges'; Black women may experience similar and different discrimination to that experienced by Black men and white women. They also experience the 'double discrimination' of sexism and racism, as well as discrimination based on the qualitatively different experience of being a Black woman (p. 63). For queer and trans people of colour they may experience similar and differing discrimination experienced by white queer and trans people and Black and brown cisgender, heterosexual people.

Crenshaw (1989) named this concept 'intersectionality', using the metaphor of the 'intersections' at which roads meet to illustrate how Black women can be located at the intersections of race and gender (and sexuality, class, etc.). Crenshaw's (1989) work draws on a long continuum of Black feminist and feminist of colour activism and scholarship which has challenged these single-axis analyses and has developed analyses that understand oppression as interlocking (Combahee River Collective, 1977; Hills Collins and Bilge, 2020). The metaphor of intersections is useful to highlight how a single-axis analysis of gender has privileged and centred the experiences of women racialised as white, and a single-axis analysis of race has privileged and centred the experiences of Black people gendered as male. The single-axis analysis occludes how systems of oppression and privilege intersect, erasing Black women and their qualitatively different lived experiences. Crenshaw (2016) describes this as an 'intersectional failure' in which Black women fall through the intersectional gap. As Lugones (2010, p. 742) suggests, 'if woman and Black are terms for homogenous, atomic, separable categories, then their intersection shows us the absence of Black women rather than their presence'; therefore, Black women 'exceed "categorical" logic'. Lugones (2010, p. 742) locates this intersectional failure within the 'categorical, dichotomous, hierarchical logic' which she argues is central to 'modern, colonial, capitalist thinking about race, gender, and sexuality'. Drawing on Maldonado-Torres' (2007) theory of the coloniality of being, Lugones (2010, p. 743) considers the gendered and sexed dimensions of the 'hierarchical, dichotomous distinction between human and non-human' forced onto the colonised in which 'hermaphrodites, sodomites, viragos, and the colonized were all understood to be aberrations of male perfection'. Lugones (2010, p. 751) describes coloniality as the

> powerful reduction of human beings to animals, to inferiors by nature, in a schizoid understanding of reality that dichotomizes the human from nature, the human from the non-human, and thus imposes an ontology and cosmology that, in its power and constitution, disallows all humanity, all possibility of understanding, all possibility of human communication, to dehumanized beings.

The classification of the human within the colonial period distinguished the human coloniser from the non-human colonised; colonised women were positioned as 'viragos' while colonised men were both feminised and hypersexualised (p. 744). However, Lugones (2010, p. 745) argues that categorically and semantically speaking the '"colonized woman" is an empty category: no woman are colonized; no colonized female are women'. Tracing these histories, Lugones' (2010) interrogation of the coloniality of gender and decolonial feminism enriches intersectionality and understanding intersectional failure through attending to the historical and social construction of gender under coloniality. She supports an intersectional analysis through calling for an 'understanding [of] the oppression of women who have been subalternized through the combined processes of racialization, colonization, capitalist exploitation, and heterosexualism' (p. 747). In reading race, gender, and sexuality through the lens of coloniality we see the interlocking nature of patriarchy, heteronormativity, and racist and colonial structures understanding the subjugation of the colonised, women, and queer and trans people as interlinked.

Echoing the work of Fanon (1986) and DuBois (2016), Lugones (2010, pp. 749, 751) describes coloniality as a 'fracture' in which the colonised must manage their own 'degradation' having been 'assigned to inferior positions and being found polluting and dirty'. This 'double' or 'third person consciousness' is troubling, in which one has a sense of self and a world of one's own meaning which is contradicted by a world that already has a meaning to impose on the colonised (Fanon, 1986, p. 111). Here Black and brown people of all genders and sexualities must negotiate how their racialisation shapes their gendering and de-gendering, sexualising and de-sexualising in which they may be hypervisible and invisible due to categorical logics of coloniality.

Intersectionality is a framework which makes 'visible the multiple positioning that constitutes everyday life and the power relations that are central to it' (Phoenix and Pattynama, 2006, p. 187). It draws our attention to the workings of power within historical contexts and the concomitant processes which shape our subjectivities and identities and that they are always intersecting, never isolated (Brah and Phoenix, 2004; Dhamoon, 2011). The subject is a 'figure of multiplicity, representing consciousness as a "site of multiple voicings" seen not as necessarily originating with the subject but as discourses that traverse consciousness and which the subject must struggle with constantly' (Brah and Phoenix, 2004, p. 78). Intersectionality rejects the essentialism and universalism of categories of identity attending to interlocking power relations and how they shape and affect our material and subjective lives. Subjectivity is marked by the violence of these power relations, and as Nayak (2015, p. 53) notes, 'racist, homophobic, patriarchal, subordinating power structures that appear as external get under the skin, into the psyche and go on to constitute Black women's self-identity in a way that is different than for white women, white men and Black men'.

Intersectionality also attends to the specificities of Black women's experience in which the intersections of racism, sexism, and homophobia 'isolate Black women from others within their communities, resulting in deep trauma, lack of support and alienation' (p. 54). I propose that a similar analysis is needed in understanding how queer and trans people of colour's subjectivities are shaped within the violence of these power relations, and how this constitutes their own understanding of self and identity. Likewise, the experiences and consequences of being confronted with the intersections of racism, sexism, queerphobia, and transphobia need to be addressed.

I concur with Nayak (2015, p. 91) when she implores critical psychology to attend to the particularity of life at the intersections and the 'emotional difficulty of embodied intersectionality'. Intersectionality highlights the existentialist dilemma experienced by queer and trans people of colour; the 'tribulations of relating across difference and transgressing externally imposed ideological, structural, emotional and psychic borders used to separate, distort, and fragment' (p. 91). The subaltern may be disorientated by navigating Western cosmology, resistance to this, and assimilation to this (through colonisation). Lugones (2010, p. 753) suggests that through inhabiting the fractures and contradictions, through living in the borders with other inhabitants, there is a possibility for the subaltern to go 'toward a newness of be-ing' taking part in 'border thinking' to create new possibilities for resistance. This draws on the work of Gloria Anzaldua (1987) and Audre Lorde (1984) to emphasise the importance of embracing difference, and 'multiplicity and of coalition at the point of difference' as a form of resistance to fragmentary, dichotomous, categorical colonial hegemony (p. 755).

Intersectionality is a key theoretical tool for understanding queer and trans people of colour's lived experience. Placing race, gender, and sexuality within the lens of coloniality provides an understanding of the ways in which Black and brown people are gendered and degendered, sexualised and desexualised at times both hypervisible and invisible, understanding race, gender, and sexuality as intersecting, colonial classifications. Framing the racialised queer, and/or trans body within the coloniality of being highlights the intersection of wider power structures: the multiplicity of oppression and degradation and the difficulties of 'embodied intersectionality' (Nayak, 2015, p. 91).

Conclusion

In this chapter I have explored the limitations of traditional psychology and charted the development of critical psychology and the different turns in the discipline which have worked to complicate research on subjectivity. For this book a turn to embodiment, materiality, and affect is integral to explore the lived experience of being-in-the-world for those who live at the intersections of minoritised race, gender, and sexuality as well as those who are of the 'majority'. Discursive psychology also remains of importance; however, psychoanalysis and phenomenology provide critical psychology with an explication of the messy, sensual life of the body.

Work from the psychology of gender, race, and sexuality has been critical in the development of critical psychology; however, having considered this work I have argued that for understanding queer and trans people of colour's lived experience there needs to be a pulling together of these threads of research. I put forward an argument for the use of intersectionality in critical psychology to pull these threads of research together using the critical lens of the coloniality of being and the work of Fanon (2007), Maldonado-Torres (2007), and Lugones (2010). I suggest that this lens is needed to address the questions of coloniality of being in the British context, and to encourage wider engagement with ideas of racialisation as foundational to subjectivity and the intersections of gender and sexuality. The psychology of sexualities and gender has made a considerable impact on the development of critical psychology; however, although there has been some critical psychological work on race and racism one may critique a lack of wider engagement with racialisation as foundational to subjectivity.

In this book I have knitted together theoretical work to develop and analyse the lived experience of queer and trans people of colour attending to how intersecting macro social structures as well as historical and political contexts shape intersectional subjectivity at the micro level. This will challenge psychology as a discipline to fully engage with structural forms of power, in particular coloniality and white supremacy and how this shapes, intersects, and co-constructs patriarchy and heteronormativity and how the subject of psychology must always be understood as intersectional. Psychology must embrace anti-/post-/de-colonial work and can no longer ignore how racialisation is foundational to subjectivity. My work unapologetically centres the minoritised and seeks to create a critical psychology that can understand the intersectional experiences of minoritisation, most importantly by and for those who are minoritised. This work is an intervention into critical psychology as well as motivated by the real need for theory and empirical research into the lives of those of us who have been subjugated and ignored within mainstream psychological accounts of what it means to be-in-the-world.

Notes

1 Quinsey, V.L. (2010). Coercive Paraphilic Disorder. *Archives of Sexual Behavior, 39*, 2, 405–410.
2 Watts, T.M., Holmes, L., Raines, J., Orbell, S., and Rieger, G. (2018). Finger Length Ratios of Identical Twins with Discordant Sexual Orientations. *Archives of Sexual Behavior, 47*, 8, 2435–2444.

4
A QUESTION OF BELONGING

Introduction

The question of belonging permeated the experiences of participants. For queer and trans people of colour there is a yearning to find community that can hold *and* embrace all their intersectional multiplicity and richness: the hope to find community in which integral parts of themselves do not have to be left 'at the door' (Yuen-Thompson, 2012, p. 420).

In this chapter, I explore the struggles participants shared in finding a place to belong – on their way to finding and creating queer and trans people of colour community. I focus specifically on the problems of belonging for QTPOC in mainstream LGBT and queer communities as well as within the wider British context in which Black and brown people navigate a structurally racist and often hostile society. I consider the tensions and fragmentary impulse of assimilationist and homonationalist discourse and the ways this positions QTPOC, problematising their place within LGBT and queer communities, Black and brown communities, and British society. These dominant discourses frustrate and complicate the search for a place to belong in all one's complexity.

There are also some silences in the chapter – what belonging looks like within Black and brown communities. In the writing of this book, I was anxious about writing about queerphobia and transphobia within these communities, and my participants tended to avoid these topics too. I was and am nervous of talking about these issues within academia, of how the white gaze already interprets our communities as pathological and inherently queerphobic and transphobic. I wanted to protect my participants, and like them, perhaps, shield our communities from further surveillance and pathologisation. Within this specific theme there is an emphasis on belonging in LGBT and queer spaces and the wider British context, and the structural forces at work on queer and trans people of colour.

However, in Chapter 6, Decolonising Gender and Sexuality, I do explore how some participants developed what I call a critical decolonising consciousness to make sense of their place within Black and brown communities and how the force of the white colonial gaze limits and constrains all forms of sexual and gender expression in these communities.

Disconnection

The experience of being on the 'outside' and not belonging in British society and mainstream LGBT and queer communities was shared across the interviews with participants. All experienced a deep sense of yearning to belong in communities with others, in community which could hold and celebrate all the complex nuances of being a queer and/or trans person of colour. Kai, a QTPOC organiser, described this as a 'trauma' experienced by queer and trans people of colour who are 'navigating different communities, trying to find a place to fit in and not finding it'.

This was reflected in Sasha's experience of feeling a 'disconnect' in her youth as a queer brown woman which made her feel 'unworthy, it made me question who I was, I didn't really understand why I didn't fit in, felt lonely'. These feelings of being out of place, disconnected, and unable to 'fit in' were internalised – with no other understanding accessible to her at the time, she experienced herself as the problem. As an older organiser at the time of interview, however, she was able to name and interpret those feelings as related to her position in the world at the intersections of minoritised race, sexuality, and gender. For Sasha it was in finding Black lesbian literature such as the writings of Audre Lorde and connecting to QTPOC communities that she was able to begin to make sense of her own embodiment as a queer brown woman. However, she had to search for these representations and connections – she notes that growing up she knew 'lots about white people' but little that was readily available to her to make sense of her own location in the world as a queer person of colour. In the Western world it is whiteness that dominates and constructs knowledge and ways of being in the world, so that all Black and brown people – queer, straight, trans, and cis – must seek out narratives in which they can understand their own lived experiences in the world.

Drawing on Ahmed's (2006) queer phenomenology, Sasha's experience of disconnection can be understood as the disorientation of not fitting in, of failing to follow the lines of white heteronormativity as a 'queer brown woman'. Sasha experiences the stress and pressure of failing to orientate around and towards white heteronormativity. This is evocative of what Fanon (1986) described as the 'nausea' of 'negation' and what DuBois described as the experience of being a problem (Ahmed, 2006, p. 139). To be negated, and to feel as if one is a problem is a feeling of being 'apart, feeling separate', as illustrated by Sasha's embodied feelings of disconnect and unworthiness which made her question her place in the world (Munoz, 2007, p. 441; Renault, 2011). However, it is through being a

QTPOC group organiser and finding similarities and solidarity in struggle with other QTPOC that she experiences a form of connection through which she can make sense of herself.

All other participants spoke to their position at the intersections of race, gender, and sexuality as well as faith and class in understanding ongoing feelings of not belonging or of being on the 'outside' (Stanley). However, for Janelle, even before coming to name her sexual orientation she had a clearer understanding than other participants that it was her race, gender, and faith as a Muslim, Arab woman that placed her as an 'outsider' in the UK. Unlike other participants, Janelle seemed to have been able to find the language much earlier to make sense of the processes of racialisation that were operating on her and how they intersected with her gender and faith. As a Muslim, Arab woman who had previously worn hijab, Janelle describes being already queerly positioned in society. The queer experience of wearing hijab as a Muslim, Arab woman in the UK is one in which Janelle was well aware of the assumptions others made of her. The hijab was a visible signifier of Janelle's difference and is invested with several different meanings and assumptions which colour the ways in which others approached her.

This queer experience could be understood as the queerness of disorientation, in which Janelle failed to orientate around and towards Western white heteronormativity (Ahmed, 2006). The hijab is imbued, by the white gaze, with questions around Muslim and Arabic sexuality. Puar (2007, p. 14) notes the two discourses at work here are 'the colloquial deployment of Islamic sexual repression that plagues human rights, liberal queer, and feminist discourses, and the Orientalist wet dreams of lascivious excesses of pedophilia, sodomy and perverse sexuality'. When Janelle no longer wears hijab, she describes being presumed to be the 'liberated Arab girl' – liberated by the secular West from the sexual and gender repression which is deemed synonymous with Islam and Arabic culture. Before even coming to 'queer' in terms of sexuality, Janelle's embodied experiences in the world as a Muslim, Arab woman engender what she describes as feelings of queerness.

Janelle is resolutely aware of the discourses related to Muslims and Arabic cultures in the UK understanding how this has shaped her experience of being-in-the-world. She describes the difficulties of being around and coming out as queer to white LGBT and straight people. She explains that

> with a lot of white people I always feel like it's jump time when I mention sexuality, it's always jump time, like, you know, or even assumption that I've left my religion, so sometimes that's their way, you know, "oh so I guess you don't identify as Muslim anymore".
>
> *(Janelle)*

Janelle describes the weight of the expectation that she must explain herself as a queer Muslim woman, and in which her sexual expression and her later decision to no longer wear hijab mean the role of 'liberated Arab girl' is enforced onto her by others.

The 'jump' or being jumped on by others about her identity invokes ideas of being under a watchful gaze, or under surveillance, that Janelle's subjectivity is reduced to one of two options – oppressed Muslim woman or 'liberated Arab girl'. This is in the wider context of continuing and increasing surveillance of Muslim communities in the UK, in which the Muslim subject has 'come to embody a "threat"' to so-called British values and security (Sian, 2015, p. 184). Janelle's experiences of surveillance in both mainstream British society and specifically white LGBT and queer spaces attest to this. The 'jump' Janelle experiences from white queers, the expectation that she is no longer Muslim as she is a queer woman, and the presumed conflict between Islam and queerness evoke the spectre of the narrative of the 'culture clash' (p. 188). This 'culture clash' is the presumption that, particularly Muslim diasporic youth will struggle to 'adjust' their British and Muslim identities – as they are positioned as in irrevocable conflict. The 'secularity' of the Western queer project sees religious practice as 'marks of subjugated and repressed sexuality void of agency' and therefore the 'agency of all queer Muslims is invariably evaluated through the regulatory apparatus of queer liberal secularity' (Puar, 2007, p. 13). Hence Janelle is assumed, on coming out, to no longer be a Muslim – because of the supposed contradiction between Islam, Arabic culture, and queer sexualities.

El-Tayeb (2012, pp. 80/81) notes that the European conceptualisation of Islam is one in which Muslims are perceived to be in 'opposition' to European values of 'humanism, tolerance and equality'. In debates about the Europeanness or non-Europeanness of Muslims, there is a focus on positioning Islam within the 'Orientalist tradition', as regressive in values particularly regarding gender and sexuality (p. 83). Yin (2005, p. 157) describes this 'dichotomy' between the Western 'humane Self' and the 'sexist, oppressive, mysterious, inscrutable, exotic, and savage cultural=racial Other'. This 'reinforcement of the Other in turn sustains the myth of the positive and normal Western Self' (p. 157; Said, 1978). The Muslim Arab is positioned as static, as holding unchangeable 'backwards' beliefs in contradiction to the universal, progressive, and changing Western self.

The 'jump' that others make to suggest that Janelle has left her faith and that she is a 'liberated Arab girl' illustrates this and highlights what Puar (2007, p. 22) described as the 'emancipatory, missionary pulses' of Western, secular LGBT movements. These movements are critiqued for their intertwinements with Western imperialism which position the racialised other as traditional, backwards, inherently queerphobic, and transphobic, positioning the West and its (white) citizens as the champions of progressive values.

Western LGBT movements are rooted in these imperialist values; therefore, as Fanon cautioned with Western feminism, we must question the impulse to separate and 'save' queer Muslims from their faith and culture, and understand anti-Muslim sentiment in the histories of those in Western European LGBT projects (Rabaka, 2010, El-Tayeb, 2012).

Janelle, however, finds relief in QTPOC spaces in which those expectations are not placed on her and there is an understanding that one

> can still be in touch with your culture, you can still be in touch with your faith and that doesn't take away from being, or your sexuality or how you identify.
>
> *(Janelle)*

QTPOC communities provide spaces in which Black and brown people can resist Western LGBT movement's tendency to fracture and colonise multiple, intersectional identities and subjectivities. Outside of QTPOC space, the intensity in which Janelle experiences the questioning of her embodied experience is such that she feels more comfortable in mainstream white spaces than queer white spaces.

> If you do speak to, or even if you don't, you know that if you did speak to them they'll have that reaction of "oh, it must be really difficult being a Muslim" and things like that, and so I, I was speaking to my partner a few days ago and I said to her "I honestly feel more comfortable in mainstream white spaces than in queer white spaces" because at least then you can kind of hide, you're already queer in being a person of colour or a Muslim or, you know, wearing a headscarf, when I did, you're already queer so you can just hide in that queerness already, whereas in a LGBT space you would hope, or you would expect, to feel more welcome and feel less like you're standing out but you actually feel a bit more, I think, because of that expectation and then realising that "oh actually I'm not welcome here" or "I'm not understood here", so that's it.
>
> *(Janelle)*

The level of discomfort Janelle experiences in white LGBT or queer spaces is such that she prefers 'mainstream white spaces' in which she is only visibly Arab and Muslim, when wearing hijab. Janelle understands her formerly visible Muslim-ness (in wearing hijab) as already queer or 'eccentric' in white straight space (Ferguson, 2004, p. 26). Therefore, being in white straight space she can 'hide' within her queerness as a Muslim, Arab woman, as opposed to managing the white queer gaze and its objectifying interest in the intersecting complexities of being queer as a Muslim Arab woman. Janelle finds some comfort and respite in hiding from the white queer gaze by being in mainstream (straight) white spaces in which her sexual orientation is less visible.

This challenges what Puar (2007, p. 15) describes as the 'powerful conviction that religious and racial communities are more homophobic than white mainstream queer communities are racist'. Janelle describes the initial shock of realising she was not welcome in mainstream LGBT space as like a 'slap in the face'. Like Fanon, she is amputated, her intricate and intersectional understandings of her subjectivity as a queer, Muslim, Arab woman were fractured and colonised. Janelle's own 'frame of reference is transgressed' as she is objectified by white queer fantasies of the Muslim (Fanon, 1986, p. xxii). She stands out in LGBT and queer space, experiencing the weight of the white queer gaze, understanding that she does not belong. As a queerly racialised subject she is an eccentricity which does not fit into hegemonic Western understandings of the queer citizen subject which orientates around white hetero- or at least homonormativity (Puar, 2007). Janelle understands this, experiencing what Fanon (1986, pp. 1111, 109) called a 'third person consciousness', how all Black and brown people experience being fixed from without by the white, colonial gaze as always knowable subjects with essentialist traits according to 'race'. Janelle is vigilant to the ways in which others limit and constrain her through static, racist, Islamophobic, and sexist intersecting lenses while attempting to see and hold onto her own sense of self. This disorientating experience is stemmed through accessing QTPOC groups, protecting herself through avoiding the white queer gaze and through a reclaiming of the queerness of her experiences.

Exclusion and 'white-washing'

Like Janelle, other participants spoke of the 'whiteness' of LGBT and queer communities; these spaces were predominantly made up of white people who dominated the space. In these spaces 'queerness' and 'transness' were coded in 'white' ways which excluded Black and brown people and there was resistance to including QTPOC and speaking about race. Participants named these spaces as 'white', clearly experiencing their racialised bodies as causing disruption and being resisted in these spaces.

The 'white normativity' of LGBT and queer communities privileges individuals racialised as white, or passing as white, and embeds 'ways of thinking, knowing, and doing that naturalize whiteness' (Ward, 2008, p. 564). Ward (2008) notes that even in racially diverse LGBTQ organisations, through whiteness white norms can continue to dominate, shaping space and racial dynamics. Bodies racialised as Other are positioned as inferior, lacking, and pathological which marks them 'socially and spatially' (Haritaworn, 2015, p. 25). Skeggs (2004, cited in Haritaworn, 2015, p. 293) argues that dependent on the ways in which our bodies are racialised we either 'move in social space with ease and a sense of value, or ... become fixed in positions and ascribed symptoms of pathology'.

Quite clearly, QTPOC experienced being fixed from without, and in occupying space in LGBT and queer communities were objects of concern and surveillance, moving through LGBT and queer space with great unease. A number of participants spoke at length about the isolation and exclusion they had experienced in 'mainstream' LGBT and queer spaces, and across all groups participants noted that their 'of colourness' was perceived as contradictory to and incompatible with 'queerness' or 'transness'.

Janelle encapsulates this by noting that in being racialised as other it was seen to be an 'extra queer thing to be queer'. Being viewed as one minority at a time, Black and brown people are constrained by the historical legacies of the white colonial gaze (Stonewall, 2012). Participants struggled with being overdetermined from without, where they are racially gendered/degendered and sexualised/desexualised in ways which robbed them of the richness and complexities of their gender and sexual subjectivities and identities. When QTPOC attempt to enter white LGBT spaces they experience a challenge to their identities – if they are to enter queer spaces it is demanded that they decide which part of their identity they will align themselves to (Yuen-Thompson, 2012). This is illustrated in Zac's experience of being asked 'are you Asian? Or are you, are you trans?'. He also noted the impulse his white friends had to 'white-wash' his identity – when he talked about race his friends claimed that they had 'forgotten' that he wasn't white. This might also be heard as being *asked* to be quiet about race and racial identity, or even demanding his silence. To be included in LGBT and queer communities QTPOC must manage the discomfort their 'of colourness' brings to a white normative space.

> Brighton is this very weird mix where if you're queer or trans, yaaay! But don't be Black or brown about it. Like you can be Black and brown and be in a picture to be diverse, but if you are Black or brown in a way that's conscious, you know ….
>
> *(Ashok/a)*

This fragmenting of identity was experienced in different ways by participants. Black (of African and Caribbean descent) participants spoke specifically about being stereotyped as homophobes and potential threats to the safety of LGBT and queer spaces, their entry to these spaces was often denied or they were questioned for entering these spaces.

SASHA: But I think that's scary like, I think (name of gay area in the city) would be scared if we, we started coming …
STEPHANIE: Can you say more about 'scared', what do you mean scared?
SASHA: Scar- cos like I think, we're, I think people, have a very kind of, certain image of what Black people are gonna be like, so, you know think, gay Black people can have an experience on (name of gay area in the city) where they don't look gay enough. Or perhaps people, doorman … are intimidated by their presence at first, so its like, oh you know can we let you in? There's that kind of, you know, an, and again in, in, linking maybe Black community with being innately homophobic and whether that's like …
ANNABELLE: mmmm (in agreement)
SASHA: gonna threaten the kind of, safe space in the context of the (name of gay area in the city)
ANNABELLE: mmmm (in agreement)

SASHA: I mean, it's not safe, but do you know what I mean? For like, perhaps that presence ... to some people threatens that...
ANNABELLE: mmmm (in agreement)
SASHA: you know, because there's all these rubbish stereotypes about Black people doing this, this, this and this.
DORIAN: Mmmmm (in agreement)

(Group X)

Sasha knows that if she was to go out in a group with other Black people to a gay bar or the particular gay area of the city, they would risk being viewed as a threat, either not being let into a space or being surveilled while there. Even in the racially diverse city Sasha lives in, she notes that the LGBT area of town purposively fails to cater for Black and brown people as the rest of the LGBT community would be 'intimidated'. Blackness is defined as a potential threat in LGBT and queer spaces and synonymous with homophobia, and this is contextualised by wider associations of Blackness with criminality, hyper(hetero)sexuality, and pathology. Hall (1978) and Gilroy (2013, p. 88) plot the development of representations of Blackness as synonymous with criminality and 'illegality', as threat to the moral fabric, and potential disorder to the civil order of the UK. Stereotypes of the Black mugger, 'the scrounger, the knifeman, the drug dealer' position Black 'law-breaking' as 'an integral element in Black culture' (Gilroy, 2013, pp. 86, 90). In Sasha's experience it is the spectre of the criminal Black homophobe that is raised by her presence. Alongside this is the fear of Black cultural expression and its inherent criminality – as seen in the racialised policing of Black club nights, music, and events such as Notting Hill Carnival (Chowdhury, 2019; Fatsis, 2019). Gilroy (2013, p. 130) calls representations of these forms of Black cultural expression, the 'Black party' and describes how they have become an 'entrenched sign of disorder and criminality, of a hedonistic and vicious Black culture' that is not 'recognizably British'. For Sasha and other Black queer and trans people, in entering the specific space of the gay bar, their bodies signify the potential for hedonistic criminality and violent homophobia. Discourses of inherent Black criminality intertwine with homonationalist discourse which set out the racialised Other as a threat to the legitimate white queer citizen subject who must be protected.

These racist perceptions mean that Black queer and trans people are deemed to threaten the very spaces which claim to be for LGBTQ people. As Sasha notes 'they don't look gay enough', they don't, or they cannot fulfil the white queer and trans norms of these spaces. Blackness and queerness and transness are deemed to be in conflict. Their Blackness means their entry is often denied or they are viewed with suspicion, and this was particularly experienced by Black men and dark-skinned Black women. One participant had been asked in a gay bar 'what are you doing here?' and had to explain that she was a lesbian.

For participants who had been a part of majority white LGBT and queer communities, they noted how they had struggled for some time before coming face to face with what Zac had described as a 'white-washing' of their experiences.

'White-washing' referred to the ways in which white LGBT spaces may include QTPOC by emphasising their sexual and gender identities while depreciating their differences in racialisation and how these intersected – an unspoken rule to fragment their identities and experience in order to be accepted. 'White-washing' is concomitant with hegemonic discourses of colour-blindness in anti-racism, in which staying neutral to or ignoring issues of race or racialisation is deemed an effective 'anti-racist' strategy. However, ignoring the material effects of race and racialisation is racism in another form and a denial of the experiences of Black and brown people. It can also be seen as an attempt to deny the histories and cultures of Black and brown communities, a demand for 'sameness' as informed by wider forces of assimilationist and 'homonationalist' discourse – as a conditional, 'ghostly', and melancholic form of belonging in the UK (Eng and Han, 2000, p. 672; Puar, 2007, p. 2).

In the UK there has tended to be an emphasis on Black and brown communities as problematic for failing to assimilate. Assimilationist discourses of the 1960s continue to echo through formal government policies (Thomas and Sanderson, 2012; Waite, 2012; Smith, 2013; Sian, 2015). These discourses reinforce the positioning of these communities as 'monolithic, self-referential and inward looking, and generative of fixed identities' (Thomas and Sanderson, 2012, pp. 162, 163). This denies Black and brown people and particularly queer and trans people of colour an understanding of their subjectivities as fluid, dynamic, and intersubjective, that allows for all complexities and reifies problematic notions of 'culture clash' (Sian, 2015, p. 188). Waite (2012, p. 353) notes an 'increasingly neo-assimilationist state articulation of belonging' in which migrants and Black and brown people are eyed with suspicion for having ongoing relationships with their countries and cultures of origin. There are "increasingly vociferous demands for undivided loyalty and affiliation to national cultures and polities" (Kofman, 2005, p. 464, cited in Waite, 2012, p. 353).

It is within this context Black and brown people navigate questions of belonging, in which they must grapple with wider forces of assimilation that attempt to discipline and fragment the complexities of their lived experience. For queer and trans people of colour wider assimilationist discourses also intersect with homonationalism which further reinforces discourses which position Black and brown communities as in conflict with the 'progressive' liberal ideals of gender and sexuality in the UK. Within British LGBT and queer communities right-wing, Islamophobic, and racist discourse is increasingly drawn upon to position specific LGBT subjects as legitimate citizens whose rights must be protected against the 'threat' of the racialised, 'bigoted', and illegitimate citizen status of the Other (Puar, 2007; Douglas et al., 2011; Jones, 2016). Queer and trans people of colour must navigate and trouble these discourses that place them at odds from Black and brown communities. Homonationalism reinforces the dichotomy of 'whiteness as a queer norm and straightness as a racial norm', in which the 'ideal queer citizen is typically white' (Puar, 2007, p. xxiv; Jones, 2016, pp. 126/127). QTPOC must challenge this binary, complicating, resisting, and dis-identifying from the limited subject positions which work to denigrate and fix Blackness and being of colour (Rage, 2016).

> Because like when, I don't know, what I feel like, when I found a place in the Brighton [QTPOC] group, and like er, familiarity as identifying as QTPOC then I had to like, come to, face to face, with all like, the kind of white washing, like … and brainwashing and erm, internalised like racism and Islamophobia for like my whole life, and most of the time, and all the time I've been in Brighton.
>
> *(Zac)*

Zac speaks to the forces of assimilationist and homonationalist impulses which pressured him to minimise his difference; turn away from understanding or naming his experiences as a queer and trans person of colour; repress and internalise experiences of racism and Islamophobia in order to access LGBT and queer communities. These pressures also existed within wider UK society. Zac describes this as 'white-washing' and even 'brainwashing', in which there is no space for his multiplicity as a queer and trans person of colour – he is either Asian or trans. This is complicated further by the very British imperative not to talk about race or racism, depreciate difference, and emphasise sameness. This is part of the British and wider European phenomenon of denying 'race' as an issue while race and racism are part of the very foundations of post-colonial British and European society (Goldberg, 2009).

To make sense of sexual and gender alterity QTPOC must make homes in unwelcoming majority white LGBT and queer spaces, while also struggling with a lack of language, resources, or support to make sense of racial minoritisation or the possibilities for a decolonising of queerness and transness. The lack of community which can hold this intersectionality means QTPOC have to fragment their experiences, making them psychologically vulnerable to the denigration of each part of themselves and perhaps more vulnerable to assimilationist and homonationalist demands to silence these parts.

Here I am reminded of Bailey, the 16-year-old mixed-race trans girl from Jones' (2016) research in a majority white LGBT youth group. Bailey was recruited into the youth group's construction of LGBT identity through 'Britishness' and therefore as a legitimate citizen through and against the local South Asian, Muslim population who were constructed as a monolithic, essentially homophobic group and therefore 'illegitimate British citizens' (p. 117). This construction was utilised by the youth to 'authenticate their own status as legitimate citizens who should not be marginalised' (p. 126). Despite not being white herself, Bailey was able to position herself within the 'in-group' as part of the LGBT youth group, as a trans girl who was importantly *not* South Asian and *not* Muslim, and therefore not queerphobic or transphobic.

Jones (2016) explains Bailey's positioning as a 'rejection of South Asian people specifically – rather than the production of a particularly white identity' in order to position herself within the in-group (p. 128). However, I would disagree and argue that Bailey is recruited by assimilationist and homonationalist discourses and the orientation around and towards whiteness, of which a rejection of the Other is key – whether that is other Others or the Other in the self. This is despite the potentially denigrating effects this may have on her as a mixed-race trans girl. Britishness and legitimate citizen status are questioned for Black and brown people, it is through whiteness and through being not-Asian in which Bailey can align herself and position herself as part of the in-group. She does not claim a white identity; however, it is through this "fierce alignment" with whiteness that she is able to belong in this space (Nayak 2003, p. 160, cited in Jones, 2016, p. 127). Whiteness itself is defined through a fierce sense of *not* being the Other.

My participants did not share this 'fierce alignment' with whiteness through racist sentiment or aligning themselves with racist discourse. However, having to fragment and silence the parts of themselves that are unwelcome or cause discomfort in wider British society as well as majority white LGBT and queer communities is perhaps on a spectrum with the assimilationist and homonationalist impulses at work in Jones' (2016) participants.

For Zac the LGBT community may have supported the development of his queer and trans identity in part; however, in meeting QTPOC and finding a space which made space for his full self he was struck by how much he had had to fragment himself by being in majority white LGBT and queer spaces and in wider British society. These spaces forced a fragmentation of his identity, encouraging further internalisation of racist and Islamophobic discourse. In creating and coming into QTPOC spaces participants were, often for the first time, able to address these experiences of 'white-washing' and begin to make sense of their intersecting experiences of race, sexuality, and gender. QTPOC groups and communities then offer the possibility of finding out who one might be when we are no longer forced to fragment ourselves and in working together to resist the forces of fragmentation. In white LGBT and queer spaces it can be difficult for QTPOC to make sense of who we may be as whole queer and/or trans people of colour, of what the intricacies of Black and brown queerness and transness may be or hold in all their intersectional richness. QTPOC groups hold the possibility of making sense of the exclusion and white-washing experienced in white LGBT and queer communities as well as in wider British society. They also hold the potential for *decolonising* gender and sexuality. I will explore this further in Chapter 6.

Race: saying the unsayable

In creating and accessing QTPOC groups and communities interviewees shared the process of beginning to find the language for their ongoing experiences of non-belonging or partial belonging as racialised, multiply minoritised people in the UK. A 'third person consciousness' was described by all participants, who experienced the negation of being the racialised other and the consequences this had on a sense of self and belonging (Fanon, 1986, p. 111).

In beginning to understand and name processes of racialisation and their intersections with minoritised gender and sexuality QTPOC challenge the ways in which Britain and the West position race and racism as 'aberrant ideological affront(s) to the enduring ideals of Enlightenment' which works to continue 'the sense of an exemplary and regulatory western civilisation' (Hesse, 2004, p. 22). Participants spoke to the everydayness of processes of racialisation and racism, and how it structures their lives in a society which denies race 'as socially, politically and indeed morally relevant' (Goldberg, 2009, p. 162). Goldberg (2009, p. 93) describes this as the European commitment to 'racelessness' in which European histories of colonialism and slavery are erased and silenced while those racialised as Other are haunted by them and the ways in which they shape and restrict their being-in-the-world.

El-Tayeb's (2011, p. xx) work on the place of Black and brown people in Europe points to the way in which 'the current construction of a European identity and history, [and] the haunting of Europe's silent racializations and ethnicizations continues to place Black and brown people outside the limits' of an accepted European community. This is particularly highlighted in Janelle's experience of being queerly positioned in relation to white queer and straight populations in the UK and in Stanley's interview in which he describes growing up mixed race in a majority white, Welsh community, and the difficulties of talking about race and difference.

Most interviewee participants spoke to the process of learning about race – that their current understandings of their location as racialised minorities in the UK had taken time to develop. The European commitment to racelessness means that, unlike places like America, language for speaking about race, and societal engagement with colonial histories of race and their legacies are absent from mainstream discourse. The three mixed-race participants (Sasha, Kai, and Stanley) had noticed their difference and experiences of not belonging but had been unable to clearly name or make sense of these experiences for some time.

The commitment to 'racelessness' made it difficult for participants to speak to and name processes of racialisation. Ashok/a, who was not mixed race, also spoke to a turning away from race – that in coming out and in being an artist they moved in white middle-class circles and actively avoided spaces of cultural origin, that even being a part of QTPOC was a way of not quite addressing their own specific racialisation. Facing race in a society that denies its place in its formation makes it painful and difficult to make sense of for Black and brown people, and this is troubled further for QTPOC who must grapple with the further alienation through intersecting gender and sexual alterity.

In the interview data, all participants, apart from Janelle, shared the slow process of making sense of their experiences of being 'different', of beginning to understand the forces working on them and the dilemmas these presented (Sasha). This could be understood as the slow sense-making of inequality, race, and racialisation in participants who were brought up within the European context of 'silent racializations', in which as children of immigrants the promise of belonging, being fully recognised British citizens, and 'home' is contradicted by experiences of alienation, exclusion, and racism (El-Tayeb's, 2011, p. xx).

These difficulties are compounded by the processes of coming out and into white LGBT and queer communities, in which those feelings of not belonging are extended. The hegemony of whiteness confuses the process of making sense of feelings of difference and, as we have seen, the lack of alternatives in understanding one's location may lead to identifying the problem with the self, as Sasha notes how she felt 'unworthy' for not belonging. Kai describes this as a traumatic process, in which queer and trans people of colour navigate different spaces unable to find a place to fit. Janelle's experience may be slightly different as a Muslim, Arab queer woman. The particularities of being a Muslim woman in the UK with its intensifying Islamophobia over the last 30 years and wearing hijab may have marked her out more obviously against assimilationist processes.

Ashok/a, Kai, and Stanley all shared experiences of having a parent they described as having 'assimilationist' values or who were 'naïve' or unable to speak of difference and race. It may be that as non-Muslims participants may have experienced more tolerance and acceptance into British culture than Janelle; however, assimilative processes left them less able to address processes of 'silent racialization' (El-Tayeb's, 2011, p. xx). As discussed previously, being instituted within assimilationist discourses may have left participants without the language to make sense of their lived experience, which may have been exacerbated by attempts to be in community with majority white LGBT and queer communities (Mama, 1995). It is in finding queer and trans people of colour community that most participants note a process of learning and finding language for their own intersectional lived experience.

> You know, and I'm not ashamed to, you know, it's the reality, very much, though, we didn't talk about race, but obviously, you still had feelings about race, you know, you knew you weren't white, of course, you know, you were almost continually made aware of that in the wider community, you know, the wider culture, I should say, as well. So, even if something isn't spoken about, you're still feeling that, you know, but at the same time there's a lot of shame and stigma about talking about difference in a way as well, you know, from people in general. So, if in school you suddenly mentioned race, even if race was an issue, there would be a kind of shutting down of, you know, "This isn't an issue, we don't see you like that", etc, etc, so not having access, really, all round, you know, to be able to talk about it.
>
> *(Stanley)*

Stanley describes the naiveté of his white family's experience with race, and the attempt to shut down uncomfortable discussions of race through 'colour blind mentality'. Stanley experienced the pressure of being continually made aware through the 'wider community ... the wider culture' that he was not white, that he was different; however, his feelings could only be shared with his siblings.

The topic of race is a site of 'shame and stigma', discomfort, and embarrassment for those around him. His embodied experience is shaped by his disorientation away from the line of white heteronormativity; however, this is papered over by those around him who wish to ignore this difference – so that he is left 'not having access' to speak to this disorientation. Stanley is told "we don't see you like that" which can be heard as a demand to no longer raise the topic of his difference. This challenges and undermines his own experience of the world – as very clearly experiencing being different and other, and that he is in fact seen *like that*.

Stanley describes the resistance to talking about race by white people as due to the topic being felt to be 'heavy' – the weight of turning to the problem of race and the racialised Other is too much to bear. Stanley describes a sense of becoming invested in not talking about race, and in becoming protective of his white family around issues of race so that he was 'oblivious' or 'tolerant' to micro-aggressions and racism until more recently. All participants highlighted the problems of being understood and belonging due to what Stanley describes as the nuances of life at the intersections in which they are constrained by the commitment to racelessness and constructions of Black and brown people's sexualities, genders, faiths, and class.

Belonging and racial melancholia

Throughout the interviews there was a pervasive sense of yearning for a place to belong, to have community in which all their intersectional richness could be held. To explore this more closely I want to turn to Eng and Han's (2000) work on racial melancholia. They take Freud's concept of melancholia, the theory of 'unresolved grief', and suggest it as a framework for conceptualising 'registers of loss and depression attendant to both psychic and material processes of ... immigration, assimilation and racialization' (pp. 669, 667).

Eng and Han (2000, p. 667) re-work the concept of melancholia specifically looking to Asian American experience, suggesting racial melancholia as a 'depathologized structure of everyday group experience'. This could be understood as a 'culturally instituted' form of melancholia (Bell, 1999, p. 166). I would argue that although their focus is on Asian American experience, this concept can be utilised to explore the problem of belonging for queer and trans people of colour in the UK.

They aim to move melancholia from the study of pathological unresolved grief of the individual to a racial melancholia which seeks to understand the feelings of loss stemming from the social and collective experiences of immigration, assimilation, and racialisation. This work follows Fanon's critique of psychoanalysis, troubling ideas of a universal psychoanalytic subject by emphasising the use of psychoanalysis in exploring embodied subjectification attuned to how the social world structures the psyche.

In the UK following immigration from the colonies and the Commonwealth since the 1950s there have been ongoing anxieties about 'Britishness' and what mass immigration may mean for the UK. Immigrants are urged to integrate and assimilate into British life, with panics and tensions arising over so-called 'ghettos', 'self-segregating' communities and unease around the success/failure of multi-culturalism. Increasing controls on immigration have become key policy within the two main political parties, and immigration has become the central topic on debates surrounding 'Brexit', the referendum on Britain's membership of the European Union. Immigrants and Black and brown people in the UK are therefore orientated towards and around assimilation to white heteronormativity; in order to gain access to mainstream culture Black and brown people must embrace 'a set of dominant norms and ideals – whiteness, heterosexuality, middle class family values' while paradoxically these are 'often foreclosed' to them (Eng and Han, 2000, p. 670).

In the West, post-Enlightenment I would argue that whiteness is equated with 'being' against non-whiteness and non-being. Eng and Han (2000, p. 670) suggest that it is the loss of the ideals, of the inability to attain whiteness or assimilation, that provides the 'melancholic framework for delineating assimilation and racialization processes … precisely as a series of failed and unresolved integrations'. Assimilation is not fully possible for Black and brown people in the UK. Assimilation is 'unresolved', engendering feelings of loss and I would suggest feelings of non-belonging and troubling one's sense of being (p. 671).

Following Freud's conceptual work on melancholia, Eng and Han (2000, p. 671) argue that in losing whiteness as something we can attain, we preserve it as a lost ideal by 'incorporating it into the ego and establishing an ambivalent relationship with it'. Keeping the lost object alive in our psyche is painful to maintain; however, in the case of Black and brown people and the lost object of whiteness this is not a pathological mourning for whiteness but one which is affirmed and re-affirmed by white heteronormative hegemony. The subject is then 'haunted' by this identification with whiteness. Eng and Han (2000, p. 672) describe this as a dangerous identification with an empty and lost object which has consequences of 'psychical erasure' of one's own subjectivity, as perhaps we can see in the participants' experiences of 'white-washing'.

The issues around belonging raised by the interview participants suggest that the imperative and orientation around and towards white heteronormativity in the UK alongside the commitment to racelessness may engender racial melancholia. As participants begin to understand the meaning of belonging and their own partial failures to assimilate, they develop an ambivalent relationship to whiteness, experiencing feelings of loss. As they begin to understand themselves as racialised minorities they must also manage concomitant feelings of loss and confusion towards their communities of origin. As first, second, and third generation of immigrants they also may carry the intergenerational loss associated with immigration. Judith Butler argues that

> the extent that the history of race is linked to a history of diasporic displacement it seems to me that melancholia is there, that there is, as it were, inscribed in "race" a lost and ungrievable origin, one might say, an impossibility of return, but also an impossibility of an essence.
>
> (Bell, 1999, p. 166)

The 'impossibility of return' for immigrants and Black and brown people and the impossibility of belonging or assimilating is a melancholic experience (p. 166). I would contend that this is further complicated for queer and trans people of colour, that these loses are further augmented by their multiple minoritisation. As illustrated, all participants described accessing or attempting to access mainstream LGBT and queer communities and found themselves further perturbed by continued feelings of non-belonging.

Research highlights the importance of LGBT communities for social support and coming to embody and accept one's sexual or gender alterity; however, participants describe these communities as failing to stem their feelings of non-belonging. QTPOC like other Black and brown people find themselves negated within mainstream society in the UK; however, this may be intensified for queer and trans people of colour as they grapple with their multiplicity and attempt to access offshoots of this society – in LGBT and queer communities – where they continue to experience exclusion.

Participants described their hopes in finding LGBT and queer communities; however, as previously discussed these were disturbed by feelings of discomfort in these spaces and participants came to name the problem as the hegemony of whiteness. Sexual and gender diversity was constructed in whiteness, and participants were unable to fit into this.

There is then a simultaneous secondary loss, at the intersection of race, gender, and sexuality. This is the loss of an assimilative (white) LGBT/queer subjectivity, as well as the loss of models of sexual and gender variance from communities, cultures, and countries of origin through the erasing processes of colonisation, immigration, and assimilation. QTPOC may be haunted by the loss of dislocation, and the 'traces of a traumatic or troubled past' (Venn, 2009, p. 10). QTPOC must manage and negotiate this dislocation and 'psychic trauma' developing possibilities for new forms of subjectivity (p. 12).

Making sense of one's difference and non-belonging is described by participants as a process which is frustrated by white heteronormativity and hegemony. It is through the often painful and arduous processes of seeking a place of belonging or home that QTPOC come to begin to understand their place in the world. This is potentially further frustrated by Black and brown claims to a heteronormative 'authenticity' (Human Rights Watch, 2008; Wright, 2013; Nguyen and Koontz, 2014). This is in part what Nayak (2015) describes as the 'torturous ambiguities' of embodied intersectionality. Kai (p. 21) poignantly describes a picture they have taken of an industrial warehouse near to their home which 'disturbs' them and invokes feelings of their own 'dislocation' and lack of a 'sense of belonging'.

KAI: This I walk home past most nights, it's round the corner from my house and what it actually is is less relevant than the picture which is like it's an industrial warehouse where they just store lots of stuff basically but it kind of ... Even though it's a really unhospitable, not very nice thing to look at, it kind of feels, there's something about it that disturbs me in that it feels really like home, like in that like it's really ... There's no way into it, like I don't, like I feel like there's dislocation of home, like I don't ever have this sense of belonging and so it, I don't know, like I look at that and I feel like myself was reflected back and I know that that sounds really emo and ridiculous but like there's something about the being on the outside and also the looking in at the vacuousness, is that a word?... Yeah, of it that makes me feel like I'm looking in the mirror ... Um, like the nothing, I don't know, like the ... Like there's something there and there's nothing here, like you look at it and you see something and you see nothing and I think, like I think on a cultural level being from London and everything then there's something really ... There's something that really speaks to me aesthetically in the kind of like griminess and dankness of it and I think that there's something really emotional in the sense of loss and the sense of nothingness and the sense of ... Like there's kind of really two things that are actually quite contradictory, like the sense of that in me but also the sense of like actually in those spaces what is is really vacuousness and I don't want anyway when I'm in them, so like whether that's queer space and like spending so many years trying to belong and then being like, fuck you, I didn't want to belong anyway [laughs] because actually when I realised what you are it's you and it's not me, even though I thought it was me .... Um, so yeah, there's something about that and then like ... But yeah, like the private property, no parking is like the gate might be open one day and I might have to go in for a short while but then I have to leave, it's not mine like and it just makes me feel really empty. Yeah ....

STEPHANIE: And so inside the gate, so it signifies spaces like queer spaces that you didn't feel you belonged?

KAI: Yeah, like all those spaces I've tried to belong that I don't belong. I feel like I'm kind of always in a space standing behind this gate, like I can look in at it and I can observe and so if there's something happening on the other side of that gate I can be part of it in a temporal sense but I'm never in. And then just that sense of what then is reflected back to me is the like, yeah, like vacuousness of my life and emptiness of non-fulfilment of things and I know that's really emo and ridiculous but ... it speaks to me! [Laughs]

(Kai)

Kai powerfully describes the experience of not belonging 'anywhere' and the feeling of exclusion, of being outside of different communities looking in. The above extract speaks to a strong sense of 'dislocation' and loss, and a yearning for belonging. There are feelings of ambivalence towards these communities – of wanting to belong, but also defiance in not belonging and a disdain, particularly for (white) queer communities.

This extract illustrates the slow process of understanding of one's place in the world and the disturbing and depressive quality to feelings of not belonging as a queer and trans person of colour. In previous experiences in white LGBT spaces Kai describes the disorientation of

> this sense of like I don't quite fit here and never really understanding why that was and then thinking it was just me, like that there's something wrong with me.
>
> (Kai)

However, at the time of the interview, like other participants, they reflected that this was related to the intersection of race and class as well as gender and sexuality.

Kai describes the disturbing feelings of the loss and emptiness which accompanies the experience of non-belonging. The warehouse symbolises an 'unhospitable' home, in which Kai simultaneously sees themselves reflected and un-reflected in, they 'see something and you see nothing'. It is a place where Kai has spent many years 'trying to belong' before realising that this space, 'what you are it's you and it's not me, even though I thought it was me'. Kai understands that they will not find a place of belonging here, after years of trying. They describe a process of trying to assimilate, of thinking that they would be able to fit into this space, that this was how they could access fulfilment. This space that they are trying to access in the wider world is also simultaneously structured within them, so that they see themselves at the same time within and not within it.

Reading this through the lens of racial melancholia, we could argue that Kai is describing the painful loss of the ideal of whiteness and assimilation developing an ambivalent relationship to these ideals. The inhospitableness and hegemony of whiteness and assimilation leaves Kai caught between attraction and disenchantment, desiring belonging but understanding that they cannot belong here. This is not a pathological melancholia but one which is structured by the social context of race, immigration, assimilation, and racialisation. Kai is interpellated as a subject who is not one. Eng and Han (2000) describe how the hegemony of whiteness and the 'social imperative to assimilate' can be understood as what Bhabha (2012) described as the 'colonial structure of mimicry' in which the colonised are instructed to mimic whiteness but are always doomed to failure (p. 676). This structures, as we can see in Kai's account, an ambivalent relationship to whiteness and a 'partial success and partial failure to mourn our identifications with whiteness ... our partial success and partial failure to mourn our identifications and affiliations with our "original" ... cultures' (p. 679). Therefore, subjectivities and identities are structured by this loss and melancholia, and ambivalence towards whiteness and assimilation.

Cheng (1997) notes that the 'melancholic condition produces a peculiarly ghostly form of ego formation' (p. 50). This speaks to the haunting quality of 'something' and 'nothing' being there in Kai's extract. It is through identification with the lost ideal that the 'melancholic takes on the emptiness of that ghostly presence and in this way participates in his/her[/their] own self-denigration' (p. 50).

Returning to Ahmed's (2006) Queer Phenomenology, Kai deftly illustrates the stress felt on the body in not being orientated around and towards white hetero- or homonormativity and middle class-ness; however, the normativity of white hetero- and homonormativity and middle class-ness makes it

> hard to understand or put your finger on what that is because there's not one big thing [laughs] that excludes you from the space and then when you don't know any different that's so internalised.
>
> *(Kai)*

The everydayness of intersectional micro-aggressions and the centrality and invisibility of white hetero- and homonormativity as the centre then make it difficult to understand one's discomfort and inability to fit.

Stanley and Sasha share similar experiences of having to search out resources to develop meaning-making and naming politically their experiences of difference. Without this language, with the invisibility of white heteronormativity, and the commitment to racelessness the social and political bases of racial melancholia become invisible (Eng and Han, 2000). As previously noted, the problem then risks becoming internalised, as Kai experiences themselves as the problem, as does Sasha. This is only something they are both able to come to terms with later through the process of connecting and building community with other queer and trans people of colour; however, the feelings associated with being excluded can continue.

A longing for home and somewhere to belong permeated all interviews. For Kai and Sasha this seemed to form in some part their motivations for their role as QTPOC organisers. For Janelle, her exclusion encouraged her to seek out these spaces, while Ashok/a described activism and friendship with other trans people of colour as providing temporary feelings of being at home.

Munoz (1999, p. 74) describes melancholia as a 'structure of feeling' and an 'integral part of everyday lives' for Black and brown people and queer and trans people of colour. Munoz suggests a reparative reading of melancholia, in that it may provide a 'productive space' in which QTPOC can 'map the ambivalences of identification and the conditions of (im)possibility' that shape subjectivity (p. 74).

The shared and similar experiences of the question of belonging as queer and trans people of colour emphasise the relational dimension of racial melancholia, the possibility of collective struggle, and a 'politics' of racial melancholia (Munoz, 1999; Cvetkovich, 2012, p. 135, 2014). This may help us in making sense of QTPOC activism and the possibilities for subjectivity it may create. However, for Stanley, older than other members of QTPOC groups, he remains on the periphery uncertain of group dynamics and more cautious of involvement, noting

> every time you feel you find your place near people, and you think, oh, you know, all queer things, then you learn, well, no, there's so much else going on, there's the same old thing going on within that group, you know, and then you're left, back to just being, you know, having to create yourself, in a way, because there isn't anything, which can be quite empowering, really empowering, but also really isolating and draining.
>
> *(Stanley)*

Spaces of belonging are created and sought out by queer and trans people of colour, navigating a world in which they do not so easily fit and in which they are positioned as the 'problem'. However, these spaces themselves can be difficult to negotiate, leaving some left to 'create' themselves (Stanley).

Ongoing feelings of unbelonging, dislocation, and a search for a place of home are threaded throughout the narratives of participants. Participants described the disorientation of being queer and trans people of colour in the UK in which they struggle with the language to name and understand their difference, while being left with the feelings of being a problem and not belonging. An understanding of these feelings is shaped by connections to other QTPOC; however, this continues to be challenged by the silences around discussions of race in the UK and within LGBT and queer communities. Participants described beginning to understand their being-in-the-world as shaped by processes of racialisation within a specific UK context which fails to recognise ongoing colonial legacies (Hesse, 2004; Goldberg, 2009; El-Tayeb, 2011). QTPOC grapple with non-belonging and the processes of racial melancholia; however, this may prove a productive part of collective struggle. In the next chapter I explore the possibilities of melancholia as a 'productive space' and the potential for connection, belonging, the erotic, and joy in QTPOC community.

5
BUILDING COMMUNITY

Introduction

Queer and trans people of colour struggle to find places of belonging, experiencing difficulties within both wider British society and LGBT and queer communities. However, for most participants QTPOC groups and connections to other queer and trans people of colour engendered a sense of belonging and an affirmation of one's embodied experience. In this chapter I explore how QTPOC groups and spaces are experienced – as places of affirmation and belonging, joy, and in which to speak back to and resist white hegemony. Drawing on the discussions of racial melancholia from the previous chapter, I consider the potentialities of what Munoz (2007, p. 444) describes as 'feeling together in difference'.

Connection and affirmation

QTPOC organisers emphasised the importance of connection in combating isolation and building a sense of belonging for queer and trans people of colour. Sasha described the group she created as a space which 'enables people to feel more confident in themselves and maybe more self-secure', and for her, knowing that there was a growing network of QTPOC groups across the UK was 'reassuring and empowering'. For Sasha, QTPOC organising provided her with a sense of community that she had always wished for. In creating an alternative space for people who are isolated and excluded within LGBT and queer communities and wider British society there was potential to stem the 'nausea' of 'negation' providing the possibilities of finding confidence, security, connection, belonging, and community (Ahmed, 2006, p. 139). It is through building relationships, connections, and community with others like themselves that QTPOC may find a possibility of 'home'.

DOI: 10.4324/9780429437694-5

In being in QTPOC groups, participants found themselves in majority spaces often for the first time. This provided a forum for sharing similar and differing experiences with the potential for affirmation and social support.

> It was just like, like it was just really exciting, being like, just being able to meet other people where like, like, most people you meet like you, you have to, like work around like explaining like something or like, I feel like, I always feel like, I have to like tread lightly around certain topics in front of say for example, if I meet a white person like I don't by default feel like I can say anything relating to my views on race, like straight away. Or like, I mean like that's the case with all QTPOC people, but I mean in general like talking about my gender, my sexuality, erm, and like related to ethnicity and race, I, you don't, like the starting point for communicating people is quite different because you kind of don't, there are some things like with most people you have to explain. Erm, so it's just, I don't know, like it's definitely, yeah I definitely feel more comfortable around other QTPOC people than like members of the general population (laughs).
>
> *(James)*

In experiencing majority space away from whiteness and straightness, participants were able to be less wary in expressing themselves and their experiences relating to race, sexuality, and gender. James described how they have had to fragment their experiences, silencing parts of themselves which trouble and are troubled by the processes of 'silent racialisation' in the UK (El-Tayeb, 2011, p. xx). There is a strong imperative to *not* talk about race, to white-wash and fragment their experiences – usually they must 'work around' and 'tread lightly' around white people in talking about their own intersectional experiences. Black and brown people are disciplined into deferring to Western liberal hegemony which constructs racism as an 'aberrant ideological affront' to British values, denying race and racism as foundational to post-colonial British society and the ways it structures our everyday lives (Hesse, 2004, p. 22). At the same time Black and brown people are positioned as backwards, traditional, and static and it is demanded that they accept the 'progressivism' of British culture. There are clear constraints on 'who can speak legitimately and what can be said with credibility' (Hesse, 2004, p. 15). As illustrated by James, participants were keenly aware of these contradictions and the ways they were limited in what could be said in different spaces, knowing that their lived experiences of race and racism challenged dominant narratives. QTPOC were conscious that they could be challenged for talking about race and their own intersectional experiences among white people and that this could be perceived as threatening. There is excitement in James' account as they experience being able to speak more freely in QTPOC spaces, here there is a different 'starting point' – one in which intersectional experiences are understood and welcomed, making James feel more comfortable than they do within the more general population.

The inhibiting effects of the presence of white people on the ability to speak to all facets of the experiences of queer and trans people of colour and the potential white response to these experiences emphasised the need for QTPOC group spaces. Across groups participants noted the dismissal of their experiences in LGBT and queer spaces dominated by white people, in which attempts to challenge this were ignored, were addressed in tokenistic ways, or resulted in heavy penalties. Being heard, having one's experience recognised, acknowledged, and validated was an important form of support across all groups.

This was echoed by Janelle's description of a 'need' for QTPOC spaces, in which her rich, intersectional life could be understood and affirmed.

> I think the first QTPOC space that I entered was just meeting that one queer person of colour and just being able to speak to someone who, without even, we didn't really delve into topics of, you know, Muslim or being a person of colour, she just understood anyway, so that was I guess my first experience of it, wasn't really a space, it was just one person, but it's just that same feeling, you know, there's less explaining to do because they already understand that it's, you know, there are more angles to it, it's not just coming out, as in sexuality, it's also dealing with whatever sort of oppressions you already deal with anyway before taking on that sexuality and, and that it's difficult and that not, and that, not just because, like it's not because you're a person of colour that you necessarily will experience queer phobia, but when you do it's a different type of queer phobia because there might be other aspects built into it like culture or religion or maybe even that acceptance of queerness isn't the same, shouldn't be expected to be the same, and it isn't the same in like I would say Muslim spaces or Arab spaces or people of colour spaces at communities I mean than it is for white people, it's very different 'cos there are other things built into it, so we cannot accept, expect them to accept it in the same way that we expected white people to accept it.
>
> (Janelle)

In meeting with and talking to another queer person of colour Janelle has a 'feeling' that there is 'less explaining to do', as they both share the embodied experience and understanding of their place in the world as queer people of colour. Together they share an implicit understanding that there are complexities or different issues which intersect with sexuality than that which white queer people may have to contend with or will understand. This is not just an intellectual understanding, but an embodied understanding or empathy shared between queer and trans people of colour.

Janelle notes that they both understand that there are 'more angles to it, it's not just coming out, as in sexuality, it's also dealing with whatever sort of oppressions you already deal with anyway'. Janelle understands her queerness as shaped and constrained through the histories, legacies, and ongoing presences of the intersections of (silent) racialisation, Islamophobia, and queerphobia. She is critical of the universalism of the Western LGBT project, reasoning that

> acceptance of queerness isn't the same, shouldn't be expected to be the same, and it isn't the same in like I would say Muslim spaces or Arab spaces or people of colour spaces at communities I mean than it is for white people, it's very different 'cos there are other things built into it, so we cannot accept, expect them to accept it in the same way that we expected white people to accept it.
>
> (Janelle)

Making sense of what it feels like to be in the world racialised as the Other and the ways Black and brown people are constrained by this supports the development of a specific knowledge of how 'acceptance of queerness' may be different in Black and brown communities. The complexity of multiple minoritisation requires a different expectation of acceptance of queerness, one that acknowledges the ways in which UK models of queerness are imbued with whiteness and how Black and brown communities already under surveillance, pathologised, and problematised negotiate difference under the pressure of white normativity and the white gaze. This will be explored further in Chapter 6, Decolonising Gender and Sexuality.

Janelle negotiates some of this by avoiding the white queer gaze. With the other queer person of colour Janelle feels she does not have to 'delve' into these topics straight away, engendered between them is a 'feeling' of shared understanding. Janelle finds comfort in these shared experiences, shared aspects of identity and being in community with other queer and trans people of colour. It is here she feels seen, with no pathologising gaze that will 'fix' her in place or claim to know what queerness feels for her as a Muslim, Arab woman.

This connection was a central part of QTPOC groups, echoing previous Black lesbian and gay groups of the 1980s and 1990s as well as in the informal community spaces around kitchen tables and in living rooms in which Black and brown queers would come together. In *Black and Gay in the UK: An Anthology* Traore (2014, p. 181) describes the informal and 'therapeutic' monthly gatherings of a group of African gay and bisexual men in London in his friend Victor's kitchen:

> Even after years of immersion in the gay scene many of us were still struggling with our sexualities and identities; and this is why Victor's kitchen was so therapeutic. We could come here with lingering questions and self-doubt, and seek others' understanding. Sometimes it was just enough to be reassured that it was ok to be Muslim and gay, or to be born-again Christian and gay. Or to be bisexual. It was fine to be different from most of our friends in White gaydom, who were often suspicious of people who expressed religious belonging too loudly.

There in Victor's kitchen with 'jolof rice, stewed beef, beer and the company of half a dozen brothers' connecting through 'similar struggles about identity' these friends were able to build community and find understanding – challenging the fragmentation of their lived experiences and identities (p. 179). Traore (2014, p. 179) described these monthly hang-outs as 'enough to restore our sanity and make us feel good about ourselves again'. This was a space in which they could find understanding and share the difficulties of navigating racism and queerphobia in the UK – of 'the endless accounts of missed professional opportunities'; the nuances of being gay or bisexual and African and how these experiences were not understood by 'White gaydom' and the complexities of 'race, sex, and desire' (pp. 179, 181, 180).

In Sasha's, Janelle's, Ashok/a's, and Kai's interviews it is the 'feeling' of being understood by other QTPOC which challenges the potential internalisation of minoritisation as a problem with the self. Instead, they can turn the lens onto the external world as a way of understanding their experiences of being-in-the-world.

> So, I think that just fed into my internalisation of things of just it's me that's the problem and it's me that's being weird and stuff so being with [their partner] and being in a relationship with another QTPOC who also hasn't come from a middle-class background and stuff like is really refreshing because we both walk into a room and you know, 99% of the time know what the other one's going to feel in that room or like we don't need to say things in explaining how we're feeling because half of it is already understood, at least half of it is already understood so we don't have to do the kind of preamble to get to the point of explanation, we just start like at like point 80% like [laughs].
>
> *(Kai)*

Previously Kai had not been able to clearly understand why they experienced being out of place, isolated and excluded within a variety of communities. They had begun to internalise this experience – identifying themselves as the problem. However, being within QTPOC spaces and then being in a relationship with another queer and/or trans person of colour Kai is able to begin to understand the 'problem' not as themselves, but as the problem of multiple, intersecting forms of minoritisation that shape and constrain how they are able to move in the world. They are affirmed further by being in a relationship in which there is a sharing of similar embodied experience as they share similar embodied knowledge and understanding of what it is like to inhabit certain spaces and places. In this relationship there is less need for a long explanation of how it feels to be a mixed-race queer, trans person and how comfortable or uncomfortable one feels. Making sense of the dynamics of social space and the feelings elicited by inhabiting the space are affirmed by Kai's partner who already understands these feelings because they experience them too.

The internalisation of the experience of disorientation is challenged by this intersubjectivity; in sharing the experience of how the skin of the social impresses on them as a queer and trans person of colour Kai's experiences of disorientation are affirmed as a problem that is social and political in its base. Here then there is a sense that QTPOC groups and relationships give some respite to feelings of not belonging, of disconnection, and of being a problem. As those formal and informal Black and brown gay and lesbian networks before them, they provide a possibility of being 'home' and of 'resistance' to minoritisation (Mason-John and Khambatta, 1993, p. 53; Traore, 2014, p. 186). They challenge fragmentary assimilationist and homonationalist impulses, building community and spaces in which QTPOC can bring their full selves strengthening the importance and value of their embodied experience and subjugated, embodied knowledges. There is room for nuance and a valuing of the rich complexities of intersectional experience, and acknowledgement of room for ongoing development of understanding and making sense of these experiences – that queer and trans people of colour should have room to define their experiences away from dominant white normativity and white LGBT and queer discourse.

The joy and the erotics of being in community

There is a joyfulness in the description of most participants' experiences in connecting with other queer and trans people of colour through QTPOC groups.

> So, that's I think one of the nicest things about being involved in activism and hopefully as well that like just our visibility like means a lot for people. I think on the Pride march this year one of the really kind of things that touched me walking through the crowd was seeing the faces of other Black people or people of colour, you know, assuming queer people of colour who were watching the parade and seeing our banner and us having, you know, just being there and there were, it's hard to describe, like a lot of their faces were just, you could tell that they were really excited about seeing us there and that it just felt really, again I'm assuming but felt, and it did for me as well to see their faces just like life-affirming I guess, like to know that there's other people. And I mean these were all people I hadn't recognised of coming or engaging with the group so it was like did they know before then or, you know, we're the only Black group within the whole of Pride. I think there were a few church groups that had larger numbers of BME [Black Minority Ethnic] people within them but we were the only group that were solely for people of colour so, like that's one of the nice things as well that, you know, I'm privileged enough to be able to be out as an LGBT person but also as an organisation to help people feel that sense of like belonging or connection or maybe momentarily but like that, not like isolation anymore. So I think like, yeah, Pride for me and I think for a

lot of people in the group was really special, for that reason anyway I think for me, yeah.

(Sasha)

Sasha experiences strong feelings of affirmation shared at the Pride march between herself and other Black people and people of colour who were watching the parade. Here a momentary connection, a possible shared feeling of excitement and joint recognition or comradery is 'life-affirming' for Sasha.

For the strangers in the crowd, some of whom Sasha notes give her the 'Black Power' fist salute, this connection is perhaps a fleeting respite from the presumed shared experience of isolation. The joint recognition through shared ethnic backgrounds, the shared histories of Black British struggle signified in the Black Power salute, and the visibility of Group X at Pride provides resistance to the impression of whiteness in the social space of Pride and on the bodies of its attendees. The Black Power fist salute and eye contact are utilised as forms of intra-racial non-verbal communication, and appropriating Mary Rowe's (2008, p. 4) work I suggest they could possibly be understood as forms of 'micro-affirmations' in contrast to Pierce's (1974, p. 13) 'micro-aggressions'. I suggest micro-affirmations could be used to describe micro-acts of solidarity and recognition the minoritised take up when they are in majority white spaces, such as smiles of acknowledgement and the 'Black nod' shared between strangers to recognise a commonality of experience and shared identity. However small the micro-affirmations Sasha experiences at Pride, she experiences them deeply as 'life-affirming', noting that the power of these momentary connections should not be underestimated.

Sasha describes other experiences in which embodied recognition of a shared 'vibe' in a club which was majority young working-class Black gay women was experienced and further affirmed her 'Black gay identity'. Similar ways of expressing oneself as a Black, gay, working-class woman elicited connection, such as speaking 'road talk', which is a localised, classed vernacular within working-class Black communities in the UK.

For Sasha, these commonalities meant that she experienced these spaces as 'a lot more relaxed' and in which she 'felt more at home' in contrast to other [majority white] queer spaces. These embodied expressions of young working-class Black gay women impress on the social space of the club engendering a shared 'vibe', here Sasha quite clearly experiences a space which extends her body and in which she does not experience the pressure of being disconnected and disorientated (Ahmed, 2006). In this club, she is 'at home'.

She also relates this relaxed experience to the space created at Group X meet-ups. Visibility as a queer brown[1] woman is important to Sasha and engenders an embodied connection to other queer and trans people of colour, a connection which is felt deeply. Sasha's emphasis on connection and community building for affirmation can be understood if we turn to Lorde's (1984) writings on the uses of the erotic. The term 'erotic' is used by Lorde to describe a way of living authentically and the deep feelings at the 'interstices of intimate and affective connection' which 'animate our human/spiritual beingness' (Moore, 2012, para 8). For Lorde (1984, p. 56), the erotic functioned in

> providing the power which comes from sharing deeply any pursuit with another person. The sharing of joy, whether physical, emotional, psychic, or intellectual, forms a bridge between the sharers which can be the basis for understanding much of what is not shared between them, and lessens the threat of their difference.

Sasha's commitment to authentic connection after experiences of disconnection and the sharing of this joy in building community forms and strengthens the bridge to others. Sasha's experiences of visibility, recognition, and affirmation also have erotic potential, highlighting the empathetic and pleasurable quality of these experiences for her own subjectivity and in building community (Moore, 2012). Similarly, Kai describes the joy in dancing with other QTPOC, and what they describe as its 'liberatory' and 'healing' dimensions. Kai emphasises the importance of dancing and 'having a really good time' with others as a way of *being* in the moment and to *be* oneself in a space with others with similar embodied ways of being-in-the-world. Building QTPOC community goes beyond political organising to dancing and having fun together which provides a sense of deep investment with one another and of love and affection.

KAI: so I think that that's really important with dance but also just having a really good time and having this really nice space that it's gone beyond just like political organising and this sense of false community about actually people that are really invested in each other and that really love each other coming together and having a really awesome time.
STEPHANIE: And can you say more about the actual movement of, you know, the dancing.
KAI: The dancing?
STEPHANIE: Why is it liberating or …?
KAI: I think like there's something about …
STEPHANIE: Or how do you feel in your body when you dance?
KAI: Yeah, I think there's like something. I think I feel awkward, but like also [pause] I think there's just something about like … What's the expression, throwing caution to the wind? Is the wrong expression?
STEPHANIE: Yeah. Yeah.
KAI: Yeah, like just being like fuck it and just like being in your body and having a great time and like I think kind of queer music, like appreciating that music together, like dancing together, like being in our bodies and just being who we are together, not really giving a shit, like … [Laughs] I don't know, like … [Pause] I don't know, there's almost like physical release, like I don't know, like all that shit that we hold in our bodies and then just letting it go.

I think as well, like for different people, it's not true for everybody but I think dance is a way through which people can express their kind of culture and their cultural upbringings and things as well so I think for some QTPOCs it's really refreshing to be in a queer space where they can bring that in because a lot of white queer space is like two steps [laughs] and shit folk music so … [Laughs] I think like being able to be your fully queer self in a space that embraces cultural identity through music, through dance, is really amazing and actually like a lot of the dance last night isn't my cultural music or my cultural dance or it isn't my ethnic cultural dance but actually being a queer person of colour in London, and this is where I find conversations about appropriation really interesting because actually a lot of the music and the dance last night is the music and the dance that I've culturally grown up with as a queer person of colour, even though it might not belong to me as like my heritage, if you know what I mean.

Kai understands community building as something which must go beyond political organising to being deeply 'invested' in one another. Drawing on stronger feelings of love and affection, Kai echoes Sasha's investment in the importance of connection with others. The joy of dancing with other queer and trans people of colour creates an affective tie in which Kai can enjoy being in their own body together with others who share similar and differing embodiment. The sharing of physical self-expression through dance is a moment of vulnerability and awkwardness for Kai while also a powerful erotic moment in which bodies come together to let go, to *be* in their bodies together and release physical tension.

The release of physical tension which Kai describes alludes to the physical, psychic, and emotional effects of the multiple, intersecting minoritisations that are held in and at the level of the body. Outside of these spaces QTPOC experience restrictions and limitations on the ways in which they can move in the world – here on the dancefloor with other QTPOC one can be 'your fully queer self'.

In these spaces QTPOC define and develop their own forms of queer culture, that embrace the intersections of their lived experiences and celebrate different cultural forms of expression through music and dance. Cultural identities are troubled here as Kai acknowledges that culture cannot be monolithic or strictly accessed only by those whose 'culture' it emerges from and conversations about 'culture' can also be reductive in relation to questions of appropriation. Culturally specific forms of music, dance, and expression are shared, reworked, re-appropriated, and imbued with different meanings. For Kai, locating themselves in a city like London acknowledges the ways in which different cultures mesh together so that relationships to different cultural forms are complicated and less clear cut as to who these forms 'belong' or engender a relationship to.

For QTPOC the sharing of cultural expression may support connection across ethnic differences, while acknowledging the relations between Black and brown communities and cultural expression in a city like London. The joy and experience of connection challenge the feelings of not belonging, creating feelings of being affirmed, and feelings of being 'home'.

Speaking back and creating QTPOC community and culture

Participants experienced QTPOC spaces as important in making sense of and challenging the everyday micro-aggressions they experienced, creating space in which to dis-identify from white (hetero)normativity. This was illustrated in the creation of shared language and subjugated knowledges to resist the drain of everyday racism, queerphobia, and transphobia and their intersections.

KAI: Then there was a discussion and one of the members who is more readily contributing started a discussion on gentrification. They had had a bad experience that day in an area of North London that they had grown up in and they were really angry. They used the group – which happens quite a lot, which I think is positive – to come and vent about it and to just get some of that stuff you were talking about, about how like important it is of people saying 'Yes, I've experienced that and that is real', da, de, da.

ASHOK/A: And it happening at the time. Not like – there is a lot of stuff that happened 10 years ago that now I have space to talk about it. I am simultaneously jealous and pleased of what all of us have managed to create in different ways and spaces where you can actually go. 'The shitty thing happened to me today' and I think that getting that at the time is much the best way.

KAI: Yes, it's really true. So what happened is that then a lot of people, mostly who knew this person, the person who posted it, so it was a kind of group of people who knew each other in real life mostly, were going through that process of kind of having a ... conversation and what happened then, and I think that I see it tends to happen more and more, is that when you are having that experience of being validated is that you become more and more flippant, because you can be and because it's accepted to be in that place. And that is a healing process. So they were saying things, like they were talking about white people and the ... of white people and things like that and angrily. And I think that that is very valid, but this particular person who had just joined said 'Hang on a minute, I kind of agree with the general point, but I don't feel comfortable with the way that we're talking about white people' ... and I think that that is an issue, because I think when you go through that process of being validated it is really empowering to be able to be flippant for the first time in ways that as a homogenous group, if people have been oppressive towards you, and to be able to turn the table on that is incredibly empowering.

ASHOK/A: Yes.

KAI: Conversely, it is very un-nuanced. And what you are talking about in that moment, and what you lose when you're in those conversations is that you are talking about system as a repression, so when you're talking about

whiteness you're talking about it as a system. And you might be using 'white people' as shorthand, generally. You know, some people will be talking about individual white people, and that is what I'm saying, but-
ASHOK/A: Also language, 'Whiteness' is an academic term.
KAI: Yes, definitely.
ASHOK/A: It's a middle class term. It is a really useful one because it does basically name the system, but I didn't grow up hearing people talking about whiteness.
KAI: No, exactly.
ASHOK/A: It's white people.
KAI: Yes, exactly. So that is exactly what was happening. And so it was one of those conversations where there was no right or wrong, it was just that the emotion of it was different for different people and that's upsetting …

This lengthy quote has been included here to illustrate the complexities of validation and support within QTPOC groups. Living within a white heteronormative society, naming, and defining lived experiences as queer and trans people of colour is to risk being told that what we have to say is illegitimate and implausible. This potentially disorientating experience is stemmed by the validation that Kai describes – that in sharing experience within the group space QTPOC can be reassured that their experiences are 'real' even as they deviate from what has been prescribed to be 'real' within hegemonic discourse. This unveiling could be described as a form of critical consciousness-raising within a group context, where sharing experiences and noting that these are shared experiences accentuate their wider political ramifications. This group space is important in making sense of the world as queer and trans people of colour together. Kai and Ashok/a illustrate how being validated in the group can lead to a process of venting and being 'flippant' about white people. They both frame this as part of a 'healing' process in working through troubling incidents and micro-aggressions. The group process of being flippant, and potentially being seen to 'generalise' and homogenise a specific group (white people) is described as an empowering process in which for once the 'tables have turned'.

This flippancy is reminiscent of Perez's (2012) reading of the 'critical flippancy' of the artist and blogger, Mark Aguhar aka 'The Call Out Queen'. Aguhar's work sought a cultural analysis of a world of white normativity and supremacy, patriarchy and heteronormativity while negotiating survival as a brown, fat, femme 'exposing the contradictions that survival requires, in particular the emotional and tactical oscillations between flippancy and heartbreak, boredom and rage' (para 9).

Through her work, Aguhar created space in which to refute and deflect the everyday assaults she experienced as a queer and trans person of colour, developing strategies that would 'flatten patriarchal and racist bullshit without diverting power from the work of brown, queer reflection and affirmation' (para 6). These strategies included cutting humour, the 'confessional, to theoretical, to capricious, to sneering', a toying with and questioning of power underlined with an 'antagonism' to whiteness and commitment to misandry (para 7).

Perez argues that Aguhar's work was guided by her embodied experiences as a queer and trans person of colour and feelings of rage, pain, boredom and search for affirmation as well as the use of critical theory, developing a 'politics that can learn, feel, and change its mind' (para 13). I would suggest that critical flippancy is used as a tool by QTPOC groups, specifically as illustrated in the above quote. Critical flippancy is a way through which queer and trans people of colour can provocatively dis-identify from white heteronormativity, challenging assimilationist and homonationalist discourse and their fragmentary, colonising impulse.

Through critical flippancy QTPOC 'work(s) on, with and against' white normativity and heteronormativity, developing critical cultural analyses of their place in the West as other and how whiteness structures white subjectivity, identity and culture in relation to them (Munoz, 1999, p. 12). To use Munoz's (1999, p. 4) notion of disidentification, queer and trans people of colour may use critical flippancy as one of many ways to survive and negotiate 'a phobic majoritarian public sphere that continuously elides or punishes the existence of subjects who do not conform' managing associated feelings of isolation, rage, shame, and intelligibility. According to Munoz (1999, p. 5) dis-identificatory performances (in this case critical flippancy) can help create 'new social relations … blueprint for minoritarian counterpublic spheres'. Critical flippancy is conveyed through a humoured affectation of boredom, disparagement, sneering, generalisation of whiteness and white people which works to create distance from white normativity and heteronormativity. Critical flippancy is underlined by a close reading, analysis, and critique of the workings of white normativity and heteronormativity – an ability required by the minority subject for survival under an oppressive majority. Critical flippancy works as part of creating a 'minoritarian counterpublic' sphere gaining space for reflection and affirmation (p. 5).

To be critically flippant troubles the cultural script that places white as superior, privileged, and as the norm while attempting to counteract being positioned as less than. As Kai and Ashok/a point out, this can be an empowering process; however, it could also be read as quite un-nuanced where the focus is on 'white people' in the general rather than whiteness as a system of oppression for QTPOC. However, as Ashok/a points out, the use of 'whiteness' is a middle-class and perhaps academised term to soften the blow of critique of white people. Critical flippancy may not work as a strategy for all; however, this illustrates the creative ways in which those minoritised from mainstream culture talk back to it in order to create space for themselves.

However, critical flippancy along with other modes of expression in QTPOC groups can also run the risk of creating strong group norms. It was acknowledged that not all QTPOC may use or want to 'read' the language of critical flippancy. Managing group dynamics across QTPOC groups was an issue across all focus groups – from managing differences in politics; racial, ethnic, sexual and gender differences; to the issues raised by friendships and intimate relationships.

An awareness of how some voices and ways of knowing may unwittingly dominate and foreclose potential wider inclusion and room for reflection was considered, particularly by organisers of the groups.

Organising and creating intersectional space for social support was a top priority; however, the lack of support QTPOC face in mainstream communities along with a lack of resources or funding created considerable pressure and circumscribed the groups' ability to do this. The further development of QTPOC communities and networks at both local and national levels was a part of all three groups' plans for the future. Group X were particularly focused on creating regional and national networks and the Brighton group were keen to build their capacity and improve Brighton for queer and trans people of colour. The London QTPOC group that the participants were a part of had already seen a proliferation of networks spring from their own group and were keen to continue this work. Group X and Brighton/London group both considered the importance of eschewing the norms of mainstream LGBT spaces and developing QTPOC culture.

> Erm, well when I went [to Group X] last time we had this really cool guy from, from the museum and so … there was a load of erm, pictures of different artefacts from the museum that he's erm, sort of putting together to do a project about how their African exhibits sort of, and from Brazil and stuff relate to Carnival and queer and trans identities. And I mean, he was actually a white guy who didn't stay for the whole group, erm, but yeah, I think it's like a really interesting space to kind of develop new theories and new ideas about culture and identity and it doesn't just have to be around, you know, (well known gay area with pubs and clubs in city) or whatever, it can be museums and bringing lots of different, different things … erm, and sort of historical, cultural, like queer stuff.
>
> *(Annabelle)*

As Annabelle illustrates, QTPOC group spaces also have creative potential in which members have a forum in which to develop their own ideas about culture and identity, further supporting the affirmation of their identities and lived experiences which are usually minoritised. Here, they can trouble the perceived heteronormativity of Black and brown communities and the perceived whiteness of queerness and transness. QTPOC groups then have the potential to disidentify with limited and fragmentary understandings of identity, decentring white normativity and heteronormativity. This creates space for social support for intersecting identities and experiences of oppression, cultivating creative developments in QTPOC culture and subjectivities. Similarly, Mason-John (1995) notes how Black lesbian networks in the 1980s and 1990s discussed different cultural histories of lesbianism to understand themselves. Dorothea Smartt created the 'Black Lesbian Support Network resource pack' which included how lesbians had existed in Africa, Asia and the Caribbean long before the arrival of the colonizers. The pack provided written proof of the existence of Black lesbians as far back as AD 500, and how some created their own societies. It destroyed the myth of lesbianism as a white phenomenon and gave affirmation to many of us who lived in isolated areas.

(Mason-John, 1995, p. ix)

In the following chapter I explore QTPOC groups and decolonising gender and sexuality more closely.

For participants across groups defining themselves, organising together and creating space for queer and trans people of colour were considered political acts of resistance. This included building community, visibility, as well as spaces for support, affirmation, and creativity. For Ashok/a and Kai QTPOC organising was part of a 'survival fight', noting how QTPOC seemed to be disproportionately impacted by disability and ill health:

ASHOK/A: And that is my story, but it is also a really common one. It is no accident that most of us are sick.
KAI: Yeah, totally.
ASHOK/A: It is not an accident that loads of us have fibromyalgia and fatigue or PTSD or depression or anxiety or–
STEPHANIE: Yes, definitely.
ASHOK/A: And we need – I think, and I am not there yet at all, because my own sense around my disability and disability politics is quite basic, but I really do think, and I have been influenced on this by people I am living with, like as queer and trans people of colour we cannot afford to not have health and disability at the centre of our politics. Even if it wasn't just because it is a good thing to be.
KAI: Absolutely, yes.
STEPHANIE: Yeah, yeah.
ASHOK/A: We are talking about a survival fight. We are talking about how to keep alive and that might mean some quite strange interpretations of health. Because it might mean looking after yourself really well, but it also might mean that yeah, it's alright to go out and get a bit fucked with your safe friend, if that's what brings you joy. Do you know what I mean? It has to be like that.

Navigating multiple minoritised intersecting identities as a queer and/or trans person of colour as well as negotiating multiple intersecting oppressions was understood to have an effect on physical health, mental health, and wellbeing. In particular, the trauma of racism was experienced as having far-reaching effects.

Both Kai and Ashok/a stressed the importance of incorporating disability politics into the intersectional organising and theorising of queer and trans people of colour's spaces and lives. Ashok/a's call for 'strange interpretations of health' echoes the focus of critical health psychology in which social, historical, political contexts must be foregrounded in understanding the 'survival fight' for minoritised populations. The overlap of physical health, mental health, and wellbeing was described as 'huge', and QTPOC groups were defined as integral to supporting the 'survival' of queer and trans people of colour through the creation of affirming spaces. QTPOC groups and networks were deemed forms of political acts/activism and a form of resistance to the oppressive status quo.

Feeling queerly raced together

The sharing of similar and differing embodied experience and subjugated knowledge at the intersections of race, gender, sexuality, class, and faith engenders erotic potential for a transformative collective experience of belonging for those who have expressed long-held feelings of non-belonging. QTPOC groups provide the potential to share and create space to collectively navigate the feelings of racial melancholia.

Drawing on Munoz's (2007, p. 443) work on 'feeling brown', we can note that QTPOC groups create space to bring together those who are queerly raced and who feel like they are a problem 'in commonality'. Munoz (2007, p. 444) argues that feeling brown is about 'feeling together in difference', an 'apartness together through sharing the status of being a problem'. Feeling brown is a way of understanding the transmission of affect, and commonality of feeling among minoritised communities which is 'partially illegible in relation to the normative affect performed by normative citizen subjects' (Munoz, 2006, p. 679).

> Feeling is meant to index a communal investment in Brownness. Brownness is a value through negation, the negation projected onto it by a racist public sphere that devalues the particularity of non-Anglo Americans. This negation underwrites racialized poverty while supporting other asymmetries within the social. Owning the negation which is Brownness is owning an understanding of self and group as problem in relation to a dominant order, a normative national affect. Brown feelings are the glue that coheres group identifications.
>
> *(Munoz, 2007, p. 445)*

The feeling of brownness is a feeling of being negated, if we look back to the previous chapter we can look to the melancholic and disturbing, depressive feelings of not belonging. Munoz (2006, p. 676) suggests that feeling brown is a 'depressive position' which 'chronicles a certain ethics of the self that is utilized and deployed by people of colour … who don't feel quite right within the protocols of normative affect and comportment'.

Munoz's work on brown feelings holds potential for understanding the sense of belonging engendered within QTPOC groups, of the shared 'angles' of understanding and experience of disorientation, and subjugated embodied knowledges that are transmitted between and among queer and trans people of colour (Janelle). It can also make sense of the feelings of sadness, loss, and melancholia experienced by QTPOC. Using Munoz's work, we can understand that the shared 'nausea' of 'negation' as queerly raced subjects is collectivised and transmitted through intra- and inter-racial 'emphatic projective identification' in which QTPOC belong together in difference (Ahmed, 2006, p. 139; Munoz, 2007, p. 445).

The collectivity experienced at Pride by Sasha, dancing with others by Kai, and 'critical flippancy' of the online group could be described as forms of 'emphatic projective identification' (Munoz, 2007, p. 445; Perez, 2012, para 9). Munoz's focus is specific to Latinx in describing this as 'feeling brown'; however, the experience of being a problem as a [queerly] racialised minority can be clearly extrapolated to other communities. Within a specific UK context, acknowledging histories of collective political struggles across racial and ethnic groups (for example, political Blackness) and QTPOC's re-interpretation of this through the use of 'people of colour' I suggest the feeling here is one of 'feeling queerly raced'. In understanding the self as negated through the intersections of multiple minoritisations and drawing on histories of non-belonging, feeling queerly raced for QTPOC can be theorised as a 'shared and historicized affective particularity' (p. 450).

Feeling queerly raced can be understood as the feeling of being different, of being negated, of not belonging. To be queerly raced one fails to orientate around white hetero- and homonormativity, which recognises the hegemonic whiteness of forms of normativity in the UK. Feeling queerly raced is to feel outside of normative modes of belonging, to feel loss and grief of histories of colonialism, slavery, and losses of the complexities of sexual and gender expression within cultures of origin. Feeling queerly raced is an affect which is transmitted across QTPOC, enabling recognition of each other and creating possibilities for spaces of belonging premised on shared experiences of non-belonging. The joy and eroticism of recognition and the sharing of feeling queerly raced speaks to the sensuality of bodies in struggle together and underlines these experiences as affective and passionate. This provides possibilities for new forms of subjectivity and identity, creating spaces of resistance to and dis-identification from coloniality and white heteronormativity and a reclamation of the potentialities for expansive, decolonising Black, brown, and 'of colour' queerness and transness.

Note

1 Please note Sasha moves between identifying as 'Black' and 'gay' to a 'brown' and 'queer' woman so I use both.

6
DECOLONISING SEXUALITY AND GENDER

Introduction

Haunted by the losses of models and understandings of sexual and gender variance in their communities, cultures, and countries of origin and struggling against discourses that position queerness, transness, Blackness, and brownness as separate, participants worked towards developing 'decolonised' understandings of gender and sexuality. This included re-readings of history to combat the erasure of sexual and gender variance in, for example, African and Caribbean history and viewing and creating artwork that provided representations of queer and trans people of colour. This chapter explores this work as well as the development of a critical decolonising consciousness, in which participants grappled with the complex histories of colonisation, immigration, assimilation, and the intersections of race, gender, and sexuality. This shaped the development of their subjectivities and how they understood the tensions around sexual and gender variance within Black and brown communities.

Developing a critical decolonising consciousness

In Chapter 4 participants described feelings of non-belonging and being haunted by the processes of 'silent racialisation' (El-Tayeb, 2011, p. xx). Being in the UK, participants were met with the erasure of their complex histories, struggling against the 'commitment to racelessness', amputated and objectified by white, queer fantasies of the racialised Other (Fanon, 1986; Goldberg, 2009, p. 93). In response to this, participants described the importance of the development of what I would call a critical, decolonising consciousness. Through this they could begin to challenge the silences around their histories and present, of coloniality,

86 Decolonising sexuality and gender

and the discourses which positioned queerness, transness, Blackness, brownness, and 'of colourness' as separate.

Sasha discussed several visits and projects she had organised with her QTPOC group. She described the importance of queer and trans people of colour accessing and occupying spaces, such as museums and galleries, that they have more traditionally experienced as 'not for them'. Experiencing art pertaining to Blackness and queerness in these spaces was described as 'empowering', compared to what was usually exhibited which Sasha described as being created for or 'retold through a white lens'.

As discussed in Chapter 5 Sasha's group had been involved in a project with a museum developing re-readings of African and Brazilian Carnival exhibits. Sasha describes this as a form of

> activism in terms of rewriting our own history or kind of decolonising it and, you know, talking about the fact that it exists and that Black LGBT people have existed, you know, like forever but maybe not with those acronyms, you know.
>
> *(Sasha)*

These QTPOC group meet-ups and external visits and projects created temporary queerly raced space, which could be understood as a tactic of survival and a collective working to resist the 'nausea' of 'negation' (Ahmed, 2006, p. 139). Sasha describes the museums and galleries as white spaces made for the white gaze; however, in naming this and in occupying this space with the group's presence and gaze they momentarily challenge this.

The focus on history – on re-telling and decolonising, as well as Sasha's discussion of group visits to the Slavery Museum in Liverpool and the work of a Black gay artist – highlights the history within which Sasha develops her understanding. Sasha's understanding is shaped by her position in history, drawing on specific histories here of Black subjugation and resistance. This encounter with the past highlights contesting discourses at work in making sense of life in the UK, as Sasha understands her own history as being misrepresented within British institutional spaces such as the museum or the gallery. She is aware of a 'white lens' in the telling of these histories. In re-telling and decolonising them Sasha resists histories 'retold through the white lens' which erase the potential for complex, queerly raced histories within which she can understand and 'place' herself.

Sasha's description of museums and galleries as spaces not for queer and trans people of colour highlights how these spaces orientate and cohere around whiteness, legitimating the 'language of Western supremacy' (Hesse and Sayyid, 2002, p. 150). However, Sasha challenges this all-encompassing reading of history, highlighting its partiality and limitation because of its location. Sasha's understanding and re-writing of history as well as Group X's collective presence in these spaces is subversive.

This is a common theme in QTPOC organising – the desire to understand what has been repressed through coloniality, of the fullness of our being including our sexual and gender expressions before the intersecting violent colonial binaries of gender and coloniser and colonised/human and sub-human were imposed (Elin Fisher, 2016). This could be understood as part of what Maldonado-Torres (2007, p. 26) describes as the 'decolonial turn' towards creating new possibilities for erotic autonomy, although Fanon (2007, p. 176) would warn us not to 'exalt the past at the expense' of our present and future.

Kai, Janelle, Stanley, and Ashok/a discuss artwork and cultural interventions created both by themselves and other queer and trans people of colour as ways in which to speak to the erasures of histories and the challenge of representation in contemporary culture. These stimulate reflection on life at the intersections and the development of a critical, decolonising consciousness.

In visiting an exhibition of the work of Zanele Muholi, a South African photographer whose work focuses on Black queer and trans subjects, Janelle is 'shocked' at the sheer number of Black and brown people represented in the exhibition. Janelle is used to 'LGBT' issues being defined as 'white' and 'British' which exclude her own existence as a queer, Muslim person of colour and of those outside of the West. Despite her own self-knowledge, the whiteness of LGBT and queer communities and movements trouble her own sense of self. The exhibition gives her space to reflect on how whiteness works to fracture and colonise her understanding of her place in the world.

During their interview, Ashok/a presented a photo of the Jean Charles de Menezes mosaic mural at Stockwell tube station. Jean Charles de Menezes was a 27-year-old Brazilian man living in London who was shot seven times in the head at point blank range by the London Metropolitan Police on the Northern Line at Stockwell Tube Station on 22 July 2005. He was mistakenly identified as one of the suicide bombers from a failed bombing the previous day. His murder was the culmination of a serious number of errors made by police, and his misidentification as a terror suspect hinged on 'vague and racist' descriptions of his appearance and behaviour – that he was acting strangely and had 'distinctive "Mongolian eyes"' (Heath, 2009, para 36; Sayarer, 2020, para 4). His brutal murder 'stands as a monument' to the ongoing struggles of Black and brown communities against police and state violence, racism, and terror in the UK (Sayarer, 2020, para 1). Ashok/a discussed their plans to create a piece of artwork related to de Menezes murder and their own understanding and critical consciousness of being-in-the-world as a trans person of colour.

> I had a very strong realization which was that if I was going to take hormones, yeah, I'd been doing, I'd been like socially living as male and gender [?? 9:37] for a while and this was the point where I was thinking about hormones and I know that because Jean Charles de Menezes had just been shot dead for essentially being a brown person with a rucksack on a tube train. And even back then I was thinking I would probably move back to

London and it took me a long time to do it but I remember thinking in spite of all the stuff of like am I appropriating this gender stuff, transness, maybe it doesn't apply to me, all these people are going to talk about male privilege and I knew there was something in those conversations that just didn't sit with me because I was absolutely like, yeah, obviously if people think I'm male stuff will be easier but the conversations about it didn't sit right and I realized later on, I know now that it was because I was only seeing white, trans and [??] people talk about this. And so, the construction of male privilege is about the world is centred around white men and you will become one and your life will loads fucking easier and there's like, it took me a long time to work out that's not the case if you're PoC, you go from being one racialized gender norm to another and yes, if you're assumed to be male, that will give you some points I guess under patriarchy. But my first thought was I'm going to look more like a young, I know I look like a young, Asian man, South Asian man with a beard and I want to move back to London and someone has just been shot dead for essentially being brown with a rucksack. And I realized all of that at once and when I started sort of talking to other people of colour about trans and gender stuff it turned out that that's not at all unusual and all the South Asian and Arab and Middle Eastern men or people to one who might appear more male at some point, had thought about that and all the Black men had thought about being stopped and searched because becoming a 'man of colour' or looking like you are a man of colour is a whole different deal. But I moved [to London] about two months ago, and it feels like a really sort of striking circular thing because now I know, because I've walked past this picture, I took a picture of it because it basically made me go "Oh", now I know that that's when I started thinking about that.

(Ashok/a)

As a trans person Ashok/a accessed trans spaces in coming to embody their own gender identity and expression; however, the conversations in these spaces didn't 'sit' well with them and this was difficult for them to understand. The white normativity of trans spaces had made it more difficult to name their own embodied experience as a trans person who was racialised in a specific way, frustrating the development of a critical queerly raced consciousness.

However, it is within trans people of colour spaces that their embodied feelings related to being perceived as a man of colour are affirmed – and that the experiences of masculinity as trans people of colour are much different to those racialised as white. Jean Charles de Menezes' murder at the hands of the police for 'essentially being brown with a rucksack' creates a critical moment in which the commitment to racelessness is very publicly challenged within the UK and for Ashok/a opens up dialogue to speak to the issues of racialisation at the intersections of trans/gender, state violence, and develop a critical, decolonising consciousness on these intersections.

All participants describe the process of coming to make sense of their embodied experiences, unveiling white normativity and coloniality and how this has fractured their own sense of selves. A critical 'decolonising' consciousness is developed as participants begin to note the erasure of their experiences and lack of representation in wider culture because of white heteronormative hegemony and how this has impacted the ways in which they could understand themselves and their communities.

For Ashok/a transitioning to more physically express masculinity is shaped by racialisation; however, as discussed in Chapter 4, the 'silent' forms of racialisation in the UK make it difficult to find space to navigate this (El-Tayeb, 2011, p. xx). Mainstream and white trans masculine spaces have a dominant narrative of transition equating to an increase in privilege, failing to address the nuances of this for Black and brown people, of state violence, coloniality and racialisation, and the complexities of Black and brown masculinity and gender non-conformity and expansiveness.

Participants' experiences in developing critical knowledges about their position in the world could be described as an unveiling, in which taken-for-granted knowledges centring white normativity and the commitment to racelessness begin to be challenged. As a QTPOC activist, Sasha reflected on the nuances of living at the intersections of race, gender, and sexuality and developing a better understanding and analysis of the ways in which race is more complex than she or her white work colleagues in an LGBT charity had previously understood. For Sasha, this is understood as part of a 'decolonising' process. An extended extract from the interview with Sasha is presented here to illustrate her understanding of the complexities of the intersections of race, gender, and sexuality.

STEPHANIE: Can you say a little bit about decolonising as well, what do you mean by that?
SASHA: So like the kind of ideas that you are taught about, the structures of other countries and who's shaping that kind of thought so, you know, I think a lot of people view certain African or Asian countries as being inherently homophobic and the kind of roots to that don't really go, they go to like religion but they don't explain how religion got to those places, they don't explain the fact that religion exists there but that country exists in a world that is, you know, ruled by white supremacy so it doesn't exist on its own. And the fact that [sighs], so I mean I guess that in terms of decolonising on my mind in that way but also kind of decolonising the kind of dominant ideas and thoughts about Black and Asian communities even in the UK. So I think like, you know, I had a discussion with a group of young Black men, all like lower class or working class young men in the college and all of them, you know, I was doing it at work and so I was talking about LGBT things and on that there was probably about twelve of them and together they were all very much against LGBT people and were saying quite homophobic things and I think I'm in quite a privileged position because I've

maybe experienced part of my life being in the same or similar communities that they've come from but perhaps like only within the past maybe year, I don't know, just come to realise where those thoughts come from. So a lot of people will say "oh Black people are homophobic" or "Black men are homophobic and it's awful" but don't understand the fact that as a Black man the expectations of you to be hyper-masculine and providing, big, beefy, strong, emotionally disconnected person who's going to fight for their family and their woman or whatever in a space where, you know, in an environment there's a lot, where they're less likely to get a job, more likely to be policed, you know, there's lots of things that are policing their identity as a Black man that doesn't give them the privilege to be thinking about, you know, the world and other people's views. So to then talk about what it might be like to be gay or to even think about that, you know, with acknowledging where they come from or where their lived experience is, a lot of people don't do that so it's like they don't really understand where some of those thoughts are coming from. So I think an example that highlights what I've said because I don't think I'm being very clear is that sometimes a lot of the workshops that I have I think other colleagues might be quite shocked or find it quite difficult to run because of the amount of kind of really quite hurtful things that they're saying and I don't think they mean it or have had opportunity to express it and really think about it, so it's like actually sometimes you need, they need to be allowed to say those things to allow a discussion about those things and they need to understand where that thought is coming from. And actually if you are, you know, a young lad that you have, all those expectations are resting on your shoulder to then, you know, think about what it might be like for a gay person in that community isn't always possible because those conversations aren't possible in that community because you can't necessarily let yourself be seen in that way or to be having those conversations because it's a threat to so much of what you are expected to be. And I think, you know, one of the young lads said to me, because they all went off and one of them stayed behind and we kind of talked about it a bit more and he said "if I was like white I wouldn't care", what did he say? "If I was rich, if I was rich I wouldn't have to care about, I wouldn't care about gay people" is what he said, "if I was rich I wouldn't care about gay people". And I thought that was so telling because it's like if you was rich you probably wouldn't be in a situation where he's in now where his masculinity and his expectation of him to be a Black man is controlled by so many other factors, if he was rich he'd have a lot more autonomy, if he was rich to have less community pressures to be a certain way, to fit into maybe a certain group of people that protect you, he wouldn't have to worry about potentially messing up all that because he'd be in a position of power, and I just thought that was really kind of telling quote in that a lot of people who look to other communities and say "they're homophobic" are in a position where they are allowed to think about things more so they're in a position where they can discuss what it's like to be gay or they can wear nail varnish as a man and not get beaten up, you know, they're very privileged and they don't understand the pressures and restrictions on other people's identity that hasn't allowed them to be able to be emotionally available in that way or to have those discussions because they can't for their safety or they can't because they just can't. So I just thought that was really interesting. So decolonising my mind in ways of thinking, you know, actually everybody comes at this from different perspective, everybody has different family, everybody has a different community and actually, you know, like he said if I was rich I wouldn't care about gay people and he also said when he was older he probably wouldn't care about it either. So it very much does speak about their, what's that saying about that young man's experience that, you know, that he could say that? So I think a lot of people write off communities without actually giving them time to speak or about, you know, he probably wouldn't have, didn't feel able to say that around the other eleven boys that had left at that point. So I think there's a lot, there's just a lot that people don't give time to or to understand doing and they probably won't ever understand because they don't have those kind of conversations or understand race in that way or realise that actually race is a massive factor in his life that is keeping, or at the minute anyway in that position, or living in an area like [majority Black area in city group is based] where that probably isn't something that's going to be talked about in the same way.

(Sasha)

Sasha describes decolonising here as beginning to question and unpick what she had been previously taught about homophobia in African and Asian countries and communities in the UK. Sasha is challenging the construction of the Global South as backwards and traditionally heteronormative and the West as a pillar of progressive values (Puar, 2008; El-Tayeb, 2011).

Sasha challenges the traditions she belongs to as a citizen of the West which have permeated her own understandings and relationships to Black communities. Here the traditions and politics of the West are unpicked in the development of a decolonising understanding; Sasha begins to place herself within and excavate previously hidden histories of colonialism, white supremacy, and religion. This shapes her understanding of her history, where once African and Asian countries and communities were believed to be 'inherently' homophobic Sasha places this reported homophobia considering a more de-colonised understanding of their histories – of understanding the complex ways coloniality shapes our being-in-the-world.

Sasha describes a much more nuanced and generous understanding of homophobia within Black communities. Through her interaction with the young men at college, Sasha's partial understanding is further developed in this intersubjective moment. Through this embodied dialogue Sasha begins to make sense of the experiences of the young Black men. It is important to note how

Sasha is invested in listening to and learning from them, despite their expressions of homophobia, which she reflects her other colleagues who are white would not be able to tolerate. Sasha perseveres, illustrating an investment in and love for Black community, rejecting discourses of inherent Black homophobia to understand how power and privilege are embedded within these displays. Sasha understands this as part of a decolonising process. This could be understood as the colonised's[1] desire to 'touch the other, feel the other, discover the other' over and against the chasms and 'profound wounds' created and perpetuated through coloniality – to paraphrase Fanon (2007, p. 28) it is the belief in the possibility of decolonial love (Fanon, 2007, p. 181; Maldonado-Torres, 2007, p. 24). As Sandoval (2000, p. 158) notes it is 'love that can access and guide our theoretical and political "movidas" – revolutionary maneuvers toward decolonized being'.

If homophobia, transphobia, and racism are structural then it must be understood that the ways in which these power dynamics and discourses are taken up, worked on, and resisted are different depending on subject location. Sasha is realising that Black and brown communities and their countries of origin exist 'in a world that is, you know, ruled by white supremacy so it doesn't exist on its own'.

Sasha highlights the effects of racialised and classed stereotypes on shaping Black men's subjectivities and how they are restricted and amputated from their own selves (Fanon, 1986). There is a heavy weight of expectation on these young Black men to be 'hyper-masculine … providing, big, beefy, strong, emotionally disconnected person who's going to fight for their family and their woman' in a world in which they are less likely to get a job in order to provide for others, are disproportionately policed by the state, and already perceived in pathological terms. Sasha suggests that this means they have less power and privilege for discussion and expression of non-heteronormative sexualities. Heteronormativity is racialised, with heavy penalties for those who do not orientate around both heterosexuality and whiteness.

The intersection of race, sexuality, and class means that these young Black working-class men are expected to perform a hypermasculinity which may include the performance of homophobia, and while this is restrictive and may cause pain to themselves and others, it also works as a potential defence against the white supremacist gaze and policing. Hall (2012, p. 279), following Fanon, notes how Black people are objectified by the white gaze and how this objectification may be taken up through self-objectification to 'alter the mode of objectification', defend, and protect the self. I would argue that the take-up of restrictive categorisations by these young Black men is invested with the energy of self-preservation and defence against the original objectification and the processes of being determined from without.

The young man Sasha speaks to alone tellingly describes how an increase in bodily autonomy through being rich would mean that there would be less pressure to adhere to these expectations, increasing his power and privilege and in which queerness would no longer be an issue. This suggests the intersecting raced, gendered, classed, and sexualised pressure to perform a hypermasculinity would be reduced. Sasha notes that the complexity of the 'pressures and restrictions on other people's identity' is rarely understood by mainstream LGBT organisations and that people 'write off communities' who are heavily minoritised and policed, without letting them speak. Sasha develops spaces within her work in which racialisation, class, histories of colonialism, and the present of white supremacy and coloniality can be reflected on with both young Black and brown people and her white co-workers, creating dialogue and theory on power, privilege, race, gender, and sexuality.

Sasha could be understood as someone Anzaldua (2009, p. 243) would describe as a *nepantlera*, a bridge who spans 'liminal (threshold) spaces between worlds'. Bridging is 'the work of opening the gate to the stranger, within and without,' an attempt to build community, and for which 'we must risk being open to personal, political and spiritual intimacy, to risk being wounded' (p. 246). In understanding Sasha as *nepantlera* we can understand bridging 'as an act of will, an act of [decolonial] love, an attempt toward compassion and reconciliation, and a promise to be present with the pain of others without losing themselves to it' (p. 246). Sasha is able to bridge her own liminality with that of the young Black men in the college as well as those of the white LGBT people she works with. This is a focused, compassionate desire to build community and reconciliation, refusing to 'write off' minoritised communities even as she risks being wounded. The young men's desire for dialogue illustrates in some sense a recognition of this bridging work, of the possibilities for understanding across difference. Sasha and the one young man who stays behind move towards each other, instead of away – by 'delving deeply' into this conflict, instead of 'fleeing', there is transformative possibility for both the young man she speaks to alone and for Sasha herself (p. 246). Through this decolonial impulse towards the other the understanding of self, other, and wider community can be transformed.

Through her QTPOC organising and youth and community work Sasha is in the process of raising her own and others' critical decolonising consciousness, challenging the taken for granted and developing a nuanced analysis of life at the intersections of race, class, gender, and sexuality. Here Sasha grapples with the ways in which Black people are dehumanised and constrained by the white gaze and histories of enslavement, of which 'ungendering…[was] a crucial component' (Lugones, 2007; Tinsley, 2019, p. 24). Through this Sasha makes sense of the performance of Black hypermasculinity and homophobia in the young Black men at the college, understanding how the wider historical, social, political, and economic context constrains the possibilities for free, creative, diverse, and expansive Black gender and sexual expression.

Sasha is beginning to develop a decolonising queer politic which grapples with the ways in which heteronormativity is racialised, and how queerphobia and transphobia have differing and complex manifestations when understood in the context of slavery, colonialism, imperialism and coloniality.

Hammonds (1994, p. 127) notes the paucity of feminist and queer acknowledgements or understandings of 'racialised sexuality'; that discourses on the sexualities of racialised groups are 'shaped by processes that pathologize those groups', which produce silences around the sexualities of Black and brown people. Maldonado-Torres (2007, p. 17) argues that 'being colonised means that life is lived waiting for the permanent possibility of one's body to be violated by another'. Sexuality is a 'central site upon which repression of Blacks has been premised,' in which Black people have been constructed as hypersexual, promiscuous, and lascivious (Crenshaw, 1992, p. 405). These stereotypes have been used to justify the systemic violence against Black people including rape, lynching, partus sequitur ventrem, reproductive injustice, anti-Black welfare policies, and the attempted destruction of familial, romantic, and loving relationships (Lewis, 2000; Hartman, 2006, 2019). Respectability politics has been one way in which Black communities have responded to the terror of coloniality and the pathologising white gaze attempting to protect Black people, particularly Black women, from being constructed as having excessive sexuality. Respectability is 'a process of policing, sanitizing, and hiding the non-conformist and some would argue deviant behaviour' of members of Black communities, a mechanism to protect Black communities and Black people from the pathologising white gaze as well as a way in which Black middle classes can access mainstream white heteronormative society (Cohen, 2004, p. 31). Homophobia may then be part of a more 'general fear of sexuality' within Black communities as part of a 'psycho-cultural response to the history of white exploitation of Black sexuality during slavery' (Ward, 2005, p. 495). This psycho-cultural response includes the traditions of the Black Church in which more literal interpretations of the Bible have supported the survival of Black people through slavery and colonialism but have reinforced homophobia and the development of Black nationalist politics which tie heteropatriarchy to the liberation of Black people (Ward, 2005).

Hammonds (1994, p. 141) argues that the "politics of silence" of respectability politics has developed into a 'culture of dissemblance' in which Black people police each other's expressions of sexuality – to guard against 'deviant sexuality … within an already pre-existing deviant sexuality'. Hammonds (1994, p. 141) notes that this culture of dissemblance makes it possible for 'Black heterosexual women to cast Black lesbians as proverbial traitors to the race'.

Similarly to Alexander (2005, p. 21) and Cohen (2004), Hammonds (1994) argues that it is the role of Black feminism to challenge and disrupt these historical constructions of Black sexualities, creating liberatory possibilities for Black sexual and gender diversity and 'Black erotic autonomy' to flourish. Maldonado-Torres (2007, p. 26) suggests that an 'erotic decolonial turn' is required as part of de-colonisation to 'shift away from the coloniality of established meanings, of sensing, of feeling, of vision, of gender and other modern/colonial conceptions of the body, as well as a rejection of the modern/colonial hierarchy of human experiences'.

However, these are not just 'discourses' that operate within Black diasporic space but are a politic shaped by the structural and paradoxical forces of the post- or, rather, neo-colonial. In her ground-breaking collection 'Pedagogies of Crossing: Meditations on Feminism, Sexual Politics, Memory and the Sacred' M. Jacqui Alexander (2005, p. 25) explores the 'continuity between white imperial heteropatriarchy – the white European heterosexual inheritance – and Black heteropatriarchy' in Caribbean neo-colonial states in their struggles for independence and mobilisation of anti-colonial rhetoric. Despite the violent colonial subjugation of indigenous gender and sexual diversity and imposition of laws against sodomy, of which the original focus was the protection of the white male coloniser from the indigenous 'savage', there is a nostalgia for an 'originary, unambivalent moment for the heterosexual founding of a Bahamian nation' in the neo-colonial imaginary (p. 48). The idea that sexual and gender diversity is a Western, and particularly US, invention positions LGBT Bahamians as antithetical to citizenship, threats to the neo-colonial state and anti-colonial nationalist movements. There is a desire to return to a time before colonialism of '[hetero] sexual purity' (p. 48). It is through 'this psychic residue, neo-colonial state managers continue[d] the policing of sexualized bodies ... as if the colonial masters were still looking on, as if to convey legitimate claims to being civilized' (p. 45). Black heteropatriarchy 'takes the bequeathal of white colonial masculinity very seriously, in its allegiance to the Westminster model of government, [and] in its belief in an originary nuclear family (which is not the dominant family form in the Bahamas)' (p. 62).

Alexander (2005, p. 71) notes the disciplining colonial joint forces of heterosexualisation and racialisation in shaping the neo-colonial subject, which constrain the possibilities for sexual agency beyond the 'imperial script'. The neo-colonial subject is burdened by respectability 'of the race', in which allegiance to the European heterosexual inheritance becomes synonymous with 'civility' and 'modernity' paradoxically embraced by neo-colonial framings of independence and anti-colonial resistance.

Caribbean feminisms, to differing degrees, aim to refute the 'state conflation of heterosexuality and citizenship', in part undertaking 'counterhegemonic memory work and building communities around mati work, kachapera, manroyals, and zami, which interrupt the state's continued adjudication of heterosexual inheritance' (pp. 27, 69). These terms 'refer to women loving women' with 'nuances ... that are illustrative of heterogeneity in the seemingly homogenous category of lesbian' (p. 339). This work is utilised to develop language for same-gender loving and desire specific to Caribbean islands, perhaps resisting recuperation into globalised Western LGBT projects.

Black and Caribbean feminist work illuminates the ways in which heterosexualisation and racialisation work in tandem as part of the ongoing project of coloniality, shaping neo-colonial state policies, the sexual politics of the Black diaspora, and curtailing the possibilities for 'erotic autonomy' (Alexander, 2005, p. 21, Ward, 2005). Erotic autonomy is a threat to coloniality and heteropatriarchy in all its forms and a move towards 'the decolonisation of being' (Maldonado-Torres, 2007, p. 26).

Sasha is developing her own understanding of these forces, and how on a micro level they shape and constrain the lives of both QTPOC and the young Black men in the college. We can place Sasha's praxis as a Black queer woman activist in conversation and in a continuum with other Black diasporic work on Black sexualities. Sasha disrupts hegemonic, Western understandings of sexuality as separate from histories of race, colonialism, slavery, and white supremacy and how they shape the present. This work is something that her white colleagues would perhaps find untenable. However, for Sasha there is a loving generosity to make space for Black youth to interrogate queerphobia and the performance of Black heterosexual masculinity, questioning the wider forces that shape and constrain how this young man understands himself. This is a reparative act, drawing perhaps on wider movements for transformative justice and community accountability – addressing harm beyond the punitive approaches of the state (Dixon, 2020). Dixon (2020) developed the transformative justice programme Safe OUTside the System Collective at the Audre Lorde Project which focused on addressing anti-LGBTQ violence in local communities. Her work emphasised the importance of building 'meaningful, accountable relationships' with neighbours and communities as the first step of addressing queerphobia and transphobia and creating safer communities as alternatives to state intervention (p. 12). Sasha's ability and commitment to facilitating difficult discussions and create temporary Black, safe space for youth is perhaps part of a loving holding to account with transformative and liberatory potential. This transformative justice approach holds potentialities for transforming the individual, the culture, and the 'power dynamics of the community' (Bonsu, 2020, p. 626).

Future research and activist work may want to further develop dialogue between the Caribbean and diaspora to create theory and praxis to address coloniality, heterosexualisation, and racialisation. This may provide possibilities for transnational solidarities, as well as, following Cohen (2004, p. 28), exploring possibilities of solidarity between heterosexual and cisgender and queer and trans Black folks to centre 'deviance' as resistance. This would provide decolonial potential for challenging hegemonic discourse and politics that continue to centre colonial constructions of Blackness as pathological; rejecting respectability politics; creating possibilities for centring those most minoritised; and building 'counter-normative space' expanding what and who is queer (p. 38).

The development of critical and decolonising consciousness has a transformative and reparative potential for understanding self and divisions within communities scarred by histories of trauma, violence, and oppression and ongoing coloniality (Munoz, 2007). This creates potential for the sharing of feeling queerly raced across divisions of gender, sexuality, and class by responding to these histories of oppression and how they have shaped our present.

A decolonising queer politic

> We created a queer world that was, and I wouldn't have thought about it this way then, but it was a fucking decolonising queer world. Little bubbles

of that, not often, but little bubbles of there's no need to have any conversations about how we're all queer or trans, or brown or Black. It just is the thing and these spaces are very fucking queer, and very fucking brown, Black, and it just is. But for me it was fucking magical, because Brighton is such a hideous racist place and, like I say, at that point the worst of the worst of hadn't happened to me. When it did, I had these people.

(Ashok/a)

QTPOC groups are spaces which resist the fragmentary and 'white-washing' impulses of LGBT and queer communities and wider British culture. Ashok/a emphasises the creation of a 'decolonising queer world' within QTPOC groups. Here queer and trans people of colour are able to develop a critical decolonising consciousness and exist without contradiction, where there was no question of the incompatibility of Blackness, brownness, and queerness and transness. As illustrated by Sasha's experience, this space supported the development of a language for the lived experiences of queer and trans people of colour – where previously there was a lack of language for the ways in which they experienced exclusion and othering. For Ashok/a and Kai a decolonising queer space created space for questioning Western LGBT paradigms such as the Western individualism of the 'coming out' process; resisting the equation of queerness and transness with whiteness; and space to imagine, create, and embrace a richly intersectional subjectivity.

Hunt and Holmes (2015, p. 156) identify a decolonising queer politic as one which 'is not only anti-normative, but actively engages with anti-colonial, critical race and Indigenous theories and geopolitical issues such as imperialism, colonialism, globalization, migration, neoliberalism, and nationalism'. This is a politic in which QTPOC de-colonise 'colonial gender and sexual categories' and resist the globalising, homonationalist impulses of modern-day LGBT and queer movements (p. 156).

Ashok/a noted that their decolonising queer politic is 'utterly intertwined' with a growing understanding of their own gender identity, working through their 'cis programming'. The critical move away from what is explicitly named as Western, colonial gender, and sexual categories enables Ashok/a to have a more open dialogue with their parents, in which their gender-diverse identity can be understood as part of their ethno-racial and cultural background as opposed to something outside of and incompatible with it. This could be understood as part of the 'decolonisation of being', in which Ashok/a is making sense of coloniality, how it has shaped their understanding of themselves and through QTPOC begin to create meaning of their gender through this decolonial impulse (Maldonado-Torres, 2007, p. 26).

However, Kai highlights that this decolonising queer politic is not clear cut and for QTPOC situated in the West, particularly in the UK, navigating queerness and transness under the Western LGBT project can make the decolonising process complex.

KAI: ... but on decolonising space, I think that I find that really difficult in these groups because I think sometimes that being queer and being of colour – there is a complexity between those when we're talking about decolonisation because in my anti-imperialist politics I think that Black struggle, for me, it's only useful if it is connected to global Black struggle, because I don't think that fighting for rights here matter if I am not fighting for global, for the value of Black and brown bodies everywhere.

ASHOK/A: Hmm.

KAI: Because essentially what I am fighting for is scraps from the table that all of my Black and brown sisters are actually the servants of and that is the problem, whereas queer community, in resistance to being ... our sexual and romantic relationships is often intertwined with a hedonism and an access to the frivolity of the Western culture, and how you marry those two things I think is really difficult. How you claim your right, as you've been denied them both as a person of colour and as a queer person, and how you maintain your connectedness to global struggle is really important. And then the intersection of decolonising the other parts of identity. So whether it's that we're working class or whether it's that we're disabled. You know, where those other identities like, I think that it comes an incredibly difficult task. Especially when you're trying to even have a community survive ... situated in London or Brighton where everything else is against it even existing (laughter) so I just find that, it can be a head-fuck, but I can sit in a room and think for hours about it and still not connect to any ... (laughter)

ASHOK/A: Shall we just leave you here?

Negotiating the intersecting historical legacies of both the oppression of racialised Others and pathologisation of sexual and gender minorities can be complex for QTPOC in the UK. QTPOC find themselves in the belly of the beast of former colonial powers, in which the fight for LGBT and queer rights is embedded in imperial, neoliberal, and (homo)nationalist Western politics (Puar, 2008). LGBT and queer rights are utilised in ongoing imperial relations defining sexual and gender alterity in static and Eurocentric ways, reinforcing the positioning of the Western liberal self over and against the traditional, backwards racialised Other. Kai grapples with how QTPOC can navigate, dis-identify, and resist recruitment into these politics and remain connected to global Black and brown 'anti-imperialist struggle'. Ashok/a's joke 'shall we just leave you here?' makes it clear just how challenging and complex these politics are. These complexities echo the struggles of politically Black and Black of African descent lesbian and gay movements of the 1980s and 1990s which sought to link the struggles faced in the British context to wider anti-colonial and anti-imperialist struggle in the majority world (Mason-John, 1995).

The decolonising queer political lens is useful in viewing the work of all three QTPOC groups – as spaces which facilitate the moving away from the hegemony of white, Western LGBT projects and ease the process of examining coloniality and the 'interlocking nature of race, sexuality and gender' (Hunt and Holmes, 2015, p. 157). This also situates QTPOC quite clearly within the continuum of politically Black, Black (of African descent), brown, and of colour struggle in the UK, as well as their international counterparts. QTPOC groups are spaces in which queer and trans people of colour, often for the first time, are able to begin to address the intersection of their racial, sexual, and gender identities away from white normativity and heteronormativity. QTPOC groups help facilitate a decolonising process in which Western LGBT paradigms and norms can be critiqued and the pathologising of Black and brown gender and sexuality can begin to be resisted. Future avenues of research and praxis may look to further interrogate the ways in which QTPOC navigate the colonial inheritance of heterosexualisation and racialisation within specific Black and brown communities. This might, for example, include exploring the utility of a politics of 'deviance' within Black communities to develop political solidarity across sexual and gender differences to make sense of the continuing impacts of coloniality on pathologising Blackness (Cohen, 2004, p. 28).

Note

1 Please note here that in English writing 'colonised's' is grammatically incorrect – cannot assign agency to colonised only coloniser: colonised's desire vs. coloniser's desire.

7
CONFLICT AND HARM IN COMMUNITY

the possibilities for the reparative and transformative

Introduction

This chapter examines some of the difficulties faced by organisers and members of the QTPOC groups in building community. Participants shared some feelings of unease around the investment on a community level in what Sedgwick (2003, p. 124) described as the 'hermeneutics of suspicion'. Organisers understood how those who are multiply minoritised having experienced trauma, pain, and exclusion may be hypervigilant to further attacks on the self. There is an understanding that for those of us who experience the brunt of multiple intersecting 'systemic' oppressions 'to theorize out of anything *but* a paranoid critical stance has come to seem naïve, pious, or complaisant' (p. 126). However, participants were concerned how this paranoid reading shapes some current formations of queer activism and how this may be detrimental to community building. In this chapter I consider the impact of paranoid readings of each other on building community alongside managing issues of conflict to more serious issues of violence and abuse. I draw on Fanon's theory of colonial violence and counter-violence to understand how organising collectively can be fraught with tension (Renault, 2011). Participants were concerned about an over-emphasis on safety and punitive strategies, such as 'calling out' and removing individuals from communities who exhibit problematic or abusive behaviours. Organisers were critical of how paranoid reading and a focus on individual vulnerability and injury seemed to structure some aspects of the groups, robbing the groups of more transformative potential. Returning to Munoz's (2006, p. 682; 2007, p. 443) work on the depressive position of 'feeling brown', I suggest that the feelings of being queerly raced are under-utilised because of the repetitive obsession with the 'unveiling of an external threat'. I propose that by focusing on the sociality of feeling queerly raced together we can resist the foreclosure of a reparative and hopeful politics, building on erotic experiences of connection and joy.

Identity politics: defining 'QTPOC'

As key QTPOC organisers Sasha and Kai spoke to the fragility of these groups and networks, alongside concerns echoed by Ashok/a of the ways in which the terms 'queer' and 'QTPOC' were changing in use to become more fixed and less fluid. All participants understood the term QTPOC as a banner or umbrella term under which all number of people could fit – QTPOC was used as shorthand for a specific community, or as Ashok/a suggested 'it's like a label to put on a room so that you can gather in that room'. QTPOC was not understood as an identity, but rather a term under which to organise and against which participants identified with and under. However, there were concerns of a shift towards QTPOC becoming an identity.

STEPHANIE: And like do you define under that acronym and how did you come to define in that way?
KAI: Yeah. Cool! Yes, I do, er … [Laughs] This feels so funny! Um, [pause] I think … I guess I do and I don't in that like, yes, I define in the way as it's useful to understand it but I also think it's just like a way to understand something quickly, whereas like I think it's since becoming a way to understand something, it's become a kind of identity and I'm not sure how useful it is to have the identity QTPOC rather than just like understand yourself as in community with other people with a similar experience. I don't know if that makes sense.
STEPHANIE: Yeah, could you say more about it, about the identity bit?
KAI: Uh huh. Like, [pause] I guess like within queer, trans, intersex people of colour, like there's so many experiences, so many different like combinations of those identities and things that like to be QTPOC is useful in terms of finding community and a way to navigate finding people with similar experiences but when it becomes an identity in of itself it like … Whereas it should be a unifying like moniker I guess, like then I think sometimes it can become erasing or homogenous of an experience that isn't a homogenous experience. Does that make sense?
STEPHANIE: Yeah, yeah, definitely.
KAI: Yeah.
STEPHANIE: Is there any like examples you could give or anything that made you think …?
KAI: I think just generally with labels, like I think that they serve a purpose in terms of bringing us together but we've got to be careful, you know, like people of colour in itself has become contentious because it was designed as a way to refer to communities that faced racism in order to like share in

our struggle, create a bigger movement of solidarity and challenge racism or white supremacy and now because people of colour became an identity in itself, there's the critique of it around like erasing Blackness as a unique experience or actually any racialised experience as a unique experience which to me isn't what I identify people of colour is about, like being a person of colour to me isn't my … It's like it has on some levels become my identity but I think that that's problematic because I think, um … [Pause] I think it is and it isn't problematic actually, in that I think that it's a term that should unify people not erase the individual, well not the individual but erase the unique experiences within it, so like I think once it becomes an identity, then for some people understanding the different experience is when the identity is left at the door which actually for me it's never been that, I've always understood it as a kind of a reference of solidarity between people who experience something similar but I feel like in … I'm not talking very eloquently! [Laughs]

STEPHANIE: No, you're fine. Yeah.

KAI: It's become … I think a younger generation have taken it on fully as an identity and there's now a backlash against that because of the way that it erases different experiences within that to different extents. But then also I think that for me, part of the reason it's an identity for me is around like being mixed race and other diaspora and not really having a strong sense of my own race identity, like I understand my race or my experience of race through racism actually, like not through having a positive racial identity, like whether that's because I'm not monoracial or whether that's about being diasporic or having an assimilationist brown parent or all of those things then my real kind of consciousness about my race is through experiencing racism and so then for me people of colour is a comfortable term because although I might identify as Indian or like mixed race Indian, like I don't have much of a connection to … I mean I have a strong connection to my Indian family but like not in terms of our culture, like that's something that they have and that I'm there to witness but was never passed onto me in a kind of like … I don't know what the word is, like practical way or something like …

(Kai)

There is concern here for the ways in which QTPOC can become used as a term which homogenises diverse queerly raced experiences of being in the world, erasing differences between ethnic and racialised communities as well as differences in sexual and gender expression. Its use also potentially hides or erases specific histories of struggle, and issues of power between and within different communities and the state.

Kai's narrative speaks to the tensions between collective work in solidarity and the erasure of specific experiences. As discussed in Chapter 2, this highlights the difficulties of keeping QTPOC as an open and fluid term compared to a fixed and static identity category and echoes the concerns and struggles Swaby (2014) has discussed in relation to the project of political Blackness. Hill Collins and Bilge (2020) note that more recent understandings of identity politics have sometimes missed the fact that identity politics emerged from collective and structural analysis, to work in solidarity across difference. 'Women of colour' was never defined as an 'ethnicity', but

> one of the inventions of solidarity, an alliance, a political necessity that is not the given name of every female with dark skin and a colonized tongue, but rather a choice about how to resist and with whom.
> *(Latina Feminist Group, 2001, p. 100)*

Similarly, political Blackness was a 'coalitional political identity' premised on solidarity between South Asian and Black people of African descent and their similar but differing experiences of British colonialism and racism (p. 85). 'Women of colour' and 'political Blackness' were not originally used as a form of individual identity but about a naming of political solidarity and intersectional, structural analysis. Ashok/a and Kai point to the use of 'QTPOC' as a useful organising tool but are wary of the ways it may homogenise diverse lived experiences.

While QTPOC have not begun to define quite so rigidly who is and who is not a queer and/or trans person of colour, QTPOC in itself may have in some groups become an identity which is defined by accepted forms of activism, analysis, community building, talk, and behaviour. However, for Kai QTPOC as an identity is also useful because of their own lack of positive racial identity. QTPOC allows them access to an understanding of their own racialised ways of being in the world which were not provided for them due to a lack of affective transmission through their family – which Kai understands as a function of being of the diaspora, being mixed race, having an 'assimilationist brown parent' and a lack of cultural tradition being passed down. As discussed in Chapter 4, QTPOC groups allow for an understanding of self and others through the 'nausea' of 'negation' (Ahmed, 2006, p. 139). Kai is then at once critical of the movement towards QTPOC as a particular type of identity, while also in some part recruited into claiming QTPOC as an identity. This illustrates the difficulties for queer and trans people of colour in understanding their lived experience in the context of the UK's 'commitment to racelessness' and the forces of coloniality and assimilation (Goldberg, 2009, p. 93). Kai is left to make sense of their own personhood without the foundation of their specific Indian community, in a country that denies race while structural processes of racialisation shape and constrain their experience in the world.

Safe spaces, paranoid readings

QTPOC as a term under which to organise hovers on the precipice as something which is useful but may (or already has) become 'stuck' (Ashok/a). Ashok/a points to the ways in which 'queer' was 'a verb, like it is a way of doing things' and has now become a 'thing' or an 'orthodox' holding similar concerns for the use of QTPOC. Sasha highlights comparable concerns and experiences, as she notes the turn towards the closing down of possibilities 'queer' initially gave her and the privileging of what Sedgwick (2003) described as a more 'paranoid' form of reading, critique, and activism. Sasha describes the changing politics of many more general queer spaces and notes a turn towards more 'controlled' environments in which language is policed, in which for Sasha 'spaces feel very delicate and like safe spaces taken to the extreme sometimes'. She goes further to describe these spaces as 'quite cotton wool type experiences where you feel like you can't exist' and describes leaving a tense queer workshop feeling 'like "my god, like I feel we can speak, breath again"'.

Sasha paints a vivid picture of experiencing some queer spaces as increasingly difficult, 'tense' spaces to be in – in which she feels like she cannot exist, reducing her physical presence to one in which she can barely speak or breathe. The political tool of 'safe space' is taken to the 'extreme' and is experienced as being 'cotton wool[led]' which is almost suffocating. Sasha explains that these spaces are designated 'safe' and emphasise 'left-wing and radical' politics which is seen as equated with what it means to be 'queer'; respecting different identities, expecting a certain way of speaking and behaviour, and with a lower tolerance for people who make mistakes regarding language or other transgressions. These spaces are more engaged in the process Sasha describes as 'calling people out' which she experiences as a part of these spaces being 'overly policed by some people'. This changing politics of queer can also be seen to be emerging in certain QTPOC spaces.

SASHA: Black queer spaces, I think there is, it [sighs], I think there are some that are like super, like even myself sometimes have to be like super-aware of maybe not saying the wrong thing and then at [Group X] I think because there's so many different types of people that actually probably don't identify with the word queer, that's a space where, you know, if someone maybe said something out of turn it would be a bit like "oh I wouldn't use that word" and you'd be like "okay, cool" and carry on, whereas I have been in other Black queer spaces where I feel like people are very up on kind of the right language to use and things and I've just felt a bit like I'm nervous about putting the wrong foot out of turn and I'm nervous of maybe the repercussions that would happen if I said that or what people might think of me, whereas I know I keep coming back to [Group X] and I have experienced it with the group in Leeds as well again there's just that kind of, people don't take things so seriously and there is just a bit more forgiveness and like if you've said something wrong someone maybe said to you "oh wouldn't say that" and it just feels like more relaxed. And it doesn't almost feel like you're being challenged, it's just a space to like explore where that had come from and perhaps why it's not acceptable to say, whereas I do feel a bit sometimes within QTPOC spaces that maybe just sometimes a bit hyper-aware of what I say or how I come across or, you know, for example I went to a QTPOC meet-up over Pride in London and wore a t-shirt that has got, um, oh an Egyptian queen's head on it, really famous Egyptian queen's head on it and I can't think, Cleopatra's …

STEPHANIE: Cleopatra?

SASHA: … head on it and it says "fresh" underneath it and I guess it is, and in my mind, and I really, and I really like this t-shirt and I feel like I'd had maybe a little bit of battle about whether it was cultural appropriation this t-shirt in that I'm not from Egypt and whether people thought that I might be just like celebrating this, you know, this image that is used everywhere and completely taken out of context and everyone uses it and I think like internally I was like "are all these QTPOC people going to be judging me and thinking that I'm culturally appropriating this thing that's, you know, she's not from Egypt and her", you know, my dad is Jamaican and I have no doubt that his roots lead back to Africa but in my head I was like "they're going to think I'm an awful person" and there's nothing in me that would, I'd never doubt wearing that t-shirt to [Group X], I'd never doubt wearing that t-shirt to the group in Leeds or to hang out with people that I know and that don't necessarily identify as queer but are LGBT people of colour. So I do feel like there is that kind of fear of how people are going to see you sometimes within those queer spaces because people are so up on politics, whereas I feel like there are other Black or people of colour spaces where it is a little bit more relaxed and that you might joke about it and talk about it a bit more.

(Sasha)

Anxieties about use of language and appropriation illustrate the fragility of some QTPOC spaces, in which Sasha fears making a mistake and the potential 'repercussions' of wearing a shirt which might offend others. The level of unease and trepidation Sasha experiences in these QTPOC groups illustrates a problematic investment on a community level in a 'hermeneutics of suspicion' in which those multiply minoritised having experienced trauma, pain, and exclusion remain hypervigilant to further attacks on the self (Sedgwick, 2003, p. 124).

Sedgwick (2003, p. 125) after Ricoeur traces the hermeneutics of suspicion within critical theory – including feminist and queer criticism, noting how it has become *the* mode of criticism with little room for the consideration of other modes which has privileged 'the concept of paranoia' in critical practice. For those of us who experience the brunt of multiple intersecting 'systemic' oppressions 'to theorize out of anything *but* a paranoid critical stance has come to seem naïve, pious, or complaisant' (p. 126).

For QTPOC this needs to be placed within the context of histories of dislocation, colonisation, trauma, and violence. Paranoid reading is not just restricted to theory; Sasha, Kai, and Stanley share in their interviews that this is a form of reading which shapes some current formations of queer activism and organising, including some forms of QTPOC activism. These participants share concerns for the emphasis on paranoid reading within some QTPOC groups, as highlighted by Sasha in the above extract. Kai describes the difficulties of organising spaces which bring together people with histories of 'trauma' from navigating intersecting experiences of queerphobia, transphobia, and racism alongside negotiating multiple, minoritised identities and the potential impacts this has on our affective lives and relationships to one another in community.

Feeling safe, managing harm

Kai understands the social, political, and cultural contexts in which QTPOC are positioned and the struggle to survive and stay 'safe'. Kai identifies that this struggle for survival does not necessarily lend itself to positive and healthy ways of being in community, finding that a 'hermeneutics of suspicion' and a paranoid reading of each other is privileged (Sedgwick, 2003, p. 124). Kai describes this as impacting the building of QTPOC community, they suggest that perhaps QTPOC can sometimes bring dysfunctional coping mechanisms and hurtful behaviour to others because of the trauma and struggle in navigating multiple forms of minoritisation. QTPOC groups may be helpful for many in supporting the navigation of identity and multiple oppressions; however, as an organiser Kai is aware of problematic dynamics within QTPOC groups which can be detrimental to community building.

Renault's (2011, p. 53) reading of Fanon's theory of violence and the 'erotic tension' in struggles of liberation against colonial violence may be helpful here. Fanon understood colonial violence to be 'retained or charged in the body of the colonized' and that the struggle for liberation is a redirection of that violence 'against its origin' (p. 53). Fanon conceptualised the 'dialectic of liberation as the dialectic of love', re-focusing love onto the '(de)colonized community'; therefore, 'anti-colonial counter-violence is at the same time detoxifying/purifying and traumatic/destructive' (pp. 53/54).

I would argue that while QTPOC groups bring the potential for belonging through a shared experience of non-belonging and of being negated, a paranoid reading alongside the complexities of retained colonial violence and the impulse of counter-violence for the purpose of de-colonisation can make organising collectively together fraught with tension. There is also the question of how the impulse for counter-violence may be directed at one another. As Nayak (2015, p. 94) notes about Black feminist spaces, QTPOC groups are often far from 'comfortable, cosy, safe and secure'. Kai describes the difficult tension of holding and acknowledging the pain of negation with how we can also build a 'healthy' sustainable QTPOC community.

KAI: like think about what it is you're doing and what the actual like legacy of that is going to be, like because it's very easy to be reactionary and to respond to things because you want to respond here and now because you're

passionate about them but like is that response, where's that response going and where are you going to end up in a year or in ten years' time with that, like I think that that's really important.
STEPHANIE: Can you give an example of that or what you mean by reactionary?
KAI: Yeah, so for example, um ... Well like on questions of like justice models, like punitive justice versus like restorative community justice kind of thing, so if within QTPOC community there's a problem and our response, you know, whether it's something like an allegation of abuse or something and our response is just to weed out the people and get rid of them in order to try and make everybody safe now, if we do that and we continue to do that then where do we end up in ten years and like I feel like we're starting to see some of that now when we look at how we were responding ten years ago to now, that we've got into this much more punitive model of justice of like kicking people out of communities and stuff and I find that really problematic so actually being much more invested in the community process to understand why people in our community are perpetrating things or just doing shit things because we all do shit things sometimes and how we can create a working alternative to the kind of punitive justice model that's enforced on us from the outside world in order to help create a healthier stronger community with healthier stronger individuals in it and I think that's particularly relevant for QTPOCs because of ... Because most of us have gone through like lots of shit growing up in understanding our identities, in navigating the worlds that we lived in, in staying safe and staying alive, you know, it's just been [?? 14.41] like just staying alive is hard enough a lot of the time as a queer person of colour and sometimes some of that shit that we go through we learn coping mechanisms that are fucked up and we do fucked up things to each other because of the trauma that we've been through and so thinking about the legacy of what we do, like having ways to deal with that that can mean in ten years we've got an overall more functioning healthy community than thinking in ten years well we've got rid of all these arseholes, but there'll still be more arseholes! [Laughs].

(Kai)

Over the duration of the research for this book there were several crises within QTPOC networks pertaining to issues of problematic behaviour and abuse, and concern with how to manage these conflicts. As Kai notes there has been an emphasis on punitive models of justice within some parts of QTPOC communities and within wider queer communities which encourage the 'calling out' and kicking out of people who exhibit problematic and/or abusive behaviours.

A paranoid reading of others' behaviours and intentions, from those who make small mistakes (such as Sasha's concern with the t-shirt) to more serious issues of violence and abuse, means that there is little or no room for reparative work (Sedgwick, 2003). As Cheng Thom (2019, p. 25) notes 'the strengths of social justice ideology are its sharp eyes and tongue', but as participants noted this can be a weakness when it comes to how we treat one another. Kai is critical of how these strategies of keeping safe collude with the punitiveness and violence of the state, challenging the development of a decolonising, queer politic.

Kai understands their role as a community organiser as supporting the development of compassionate, responsible ways of being in community that emphasise trust and communal wellbeing. They draw on emerging discussions within Black feminist, feminist of colour, and queer communities about how to deal with conflict and violence in ways which resist 'idealized, protectionist notions of community that purport to lessen intra-community violence', challenging the 'dominant liberal rights discourse that demands laws and legislation championing individual benefits or protections while affirming violent state structures' (Durazo et al., 2012, para 17). These critiques challenge the 'policing response to people who perpetrate violence' within domestic violence and feminist anti-violence organisations (Kim, 2012, p. 16). Kim (2012, p. 17) argues that these movements and organisations have been 'demobilized through professionalization and had become deradicalised through its pursuit of policies that were also championed by proponents of neoliberalism, most notably, criminalization'. Movements for transformative justice and community accountability are 'sensitive to avoid replicating punitive and carceral logics, which are inherently racist, classist, homophobic, transphobic and misogynist', seeking to make conflicts 'generative' in order to transform individuals, relationships, and the 'culture and power dynamics of the community' (Bonsu, 2020, p. 35).

It could then be argued that the difficulties Kai and Sasha describe in QTPOC communities may draw from the hegemonic (neo)liberal rights discourse which demands that the individual be protected from harm, and the potential problematics of QTPOC, or feeling queerly raced becoming 'stuck' in which the focus is only on negation, or what becomes an identity of injury (Brown, 1995; Durazo et al., 2012, p. 17).

> Or I think that there's this feeling, particularly with younger QTPOCs that there's this kind of you're either with me or you're against me kind of thing and the feeling of you're against me is that you don't understand how progressive my thought is and I think with [name of friend] and other, you know, a few other people, [laughs] that there's this understanding that we've kind of been through that politics and we're now critical of some of that stuff but not because, not for the reasons that ... I'm trying to explain it in a like ... So like with community accountability, the topic of the day, but like community accountability things and so like challenging the way that they're handling an incident isn't because we're part of the status quo who thinks that we shouldn't address these issues, it's because we're critical of the way we're addressing them and what can then happen is that you get called a rape apologist [laughs] or that you don't understand, you know, like that to be critical you're seen as part of the status quo and actually there's this deeper and more nuanced conversation that challenges that but

challenges the colonisation and the colonised thinking that we bring in in all of us as Western socialised people into things and trying to really deconstruct that and not just deconstruct it on the surface level and say look, claim this like new identity of being decolonial or like whatever that I think a lot of people who claim that identity as an identity which to me is just bizarre but who aren't really unpicking what that means, like with [friend's name] I feel like there's, you know, and my other friends there's like, some of my other friends there's this ability to unpick that or on community accountability and things and that to me is like I can breathe, like I can breathe with this person.

(Kai)

Kai emphasises the need for critical reflection on the modes of actions and reactions QTPOC undertake, understanding how they are shaped by colonised thinking as 'Western socialised people'. However, they also run the risk of a backlash for saying so – with younger members of the community 'there's this kind of you're either with me or you're against me kind of thing' which can be stifling and silencing. In spaces committed to community accountability, Kai, like Sasha, feels able to 'breathe'. Spaces which centre these transformative and generative dynamics potentially feel safer and less restrictive, because they are steeped in trust and a loving reparative move towards each other, rather than a paranoid moving away.

The problematics of paranoid readings of each other clearly run through some QTPOC groups threatening the building of community, with the threat of punitive actions against those who question established ways of responding to harm. An example alluded to by Kai is the case of one member of a QTPOC group who suggested running a community accountability process for another member of the community who had been accused of sexual assault. The person who suggested the process was lambasted by another member for focusing on the person who did harm and not the victim of the assault and was called a 'rape apologist' (Kai). This foreclosed any discussion of a meaningful, restorative attempt of community accountability; a much more retributive and punitive mode of addressing this harm was taken in which the person who did harm was removed and banned from a number of group spaces, and close friends of this person were asked to cut ties.

The ways in which some QTPOC group members, particularly younger people, responded to one another emphasise the problems of focusing on the self as vulnerable and injured, and a paranoid relation to others within a neoliberal rights discourse. As highlighted by both Kai and Sasha, punitive responses were not limited to people who had been abusive but were potentially directed at those who questioned ways of dealing with them, as well as those who caused offense or made mistakes, illustrated in Sasha's anxiety over her t-shirt.

However, Sasha distinguishes between these QTPOC groups and groups such as Group X which are a welcome respite from the tensions of these spaces. In Group X the bodily expressions of queer and trans people of colour are policed less with louder and freer modes of communication and a more relaxed and forgiving approach to the use of language and potential offense. Sasha understands this as in part to do with the make-up of Group X, in which up to half of the members are not from the UK or Europe which means there is more appreciation for difference in ways of relating and that although describing themselves as a 'queer' and 'QTPOC' group, Group X have differing group norms than other QTPOC groups.

Uses of the erotic: feeling queerly raced together

In returning to Lorde's (1984) 'Uses of the Erotic', Moore (2012) challenges us to question the ways in which activism is undertaken within a neoliberal era which she describes as a 'theater of disengagement' (para 6). She suggests connection and communities in struggle are undermined by this disengagement as we begin to see ourselves as objects in struggle as opposed to people with complex subjectivities in *collective* struggle which robs us of the potential of the erotic and its utility in connecting across difference.

Sasha's experiences of other queer spaces as being very controlled and policed may point towards the ways in which neoliberal ideology can affect activist organising with its focus on the individual, surveillance, safety, and authoritarian control. Sasha and Kai's experiences of these spaces also open questions of what it may mean to come together through shared experiences of negation, injury, and harm and how this structures forms of activism.

Munoz (2006, p. 682), following Sedgwick (2003), highlights the privileging of paranoid critique – that it has 'become routine rather than critical thinking', and more widely there is an obsession with the 'unveiling of an external threat'. This permeates queer communities, through which 'our relational potentiality is diminished' (p. 683). Drawing from Spillers (2003), Munoz (2006, p. 675; 2007, p. 444) suggests the generative potential of orientating ourselves towards Black and brown communities in ways that resist paranoid critique, an ethical position which taps into what he describes as 'feeling brown, feeling down' together, of 'feeling together in difference'. Munoz (2006) emphasises the 'affective particularity' of feeling brown, which I suggest here as feeling queerly raced, as going beyond identity to what it is like to feel together as 'minoritarian subjects'. This provides possibilities for the collective and a potential ethics for relating to one another, resisting the paranoid-schizoid position, and moving towards a depressive position which can be reparative. This provides possibilities for generative conflict and collective struggle, centring a politics of love – drawing from the erotics of feeling together in difference.

We must take heed that it is in the keeping alive of the depressive position, a focus on the sociality of brown feelings and feeling queerly raced, in which the individual and the collective can resist the foreclosure of a reparative and hopeful politics (p. 687). It is clear from Sasha and Kai's erotic experiences of connection and joy within QTPOC activism that there are possibilities for the reparative;

however, the potentialities of feeling brown and feeling queerly raced together may sometimes be under-utilised.

Future praxis and research may want to explore ways in which the erotics of feeling together in difference can be nurtured and utilised; consider the ways in which trauma and oppression shape the culture of activist movements and generously challenge them; and continue work to develop transformative approaches to conflict to strengthen QTPOC communities and activism.

8
CONCLUSION

In this book, I have explored the lived experiences of queer and trans people of colour and their involvement in QTPOC activism. I have explored what QTPOC activism means in the UK context, how it operates, and for what purpose; the ways in which QTPOC activisms support the negotiation and affirmation of experiences of multiple, intersecting forms of minoritisation and navigation of racism, queerphobia, and transphobia; and how personal involvement with QTPOC activisms shapes subjectivity.

The research has been firmly situated within the British 'post-colonial' context and QTPOC activism has been framed within South Asian, African, African Caribbean, and politically Black histories of resistance and struggle particular to the British context. Following Johnson (2015) I have worked to knit together these wider historical, social, and political contexts and how they may shape subjectivity with critical theory from queer, Black feminist, and de-/anti-/post-colonial theory to attend to the embodied, feeling, experience of being-in-the-world for QTPOC.

I have developed this from a critical psychological perspective, and inspired by Fanon's (1986) ground-breaking, but marginalised, work, I have aimed to emphasise how the macro-social structures and shapes subjectivity, drawing on the concepts of coloniality and intersectionality to understand queer and trans people of colour's lived experience. I have been increasingly influenced by Johnson's (2015) turn to the psychosocial and reparative. Following Sedgwick's (2003) reparative turn, Johnson (2015, p. 176) has encouraged a focus on inter-subjectivity, feeling, experience, ontology, and community promoting a trans-disciplinary approach to 'reimagine the psychological'.

Inspired by the possibilities of a transdisciplinary approach, I have drawn on the work of Munoz (1999, 2006, 2007), Mama (1995), Nayak (2015),

Butler (1997), Fanon (1986), Ahmed (2006), Phoenix (2013), Lewis (2000), Quijano (2007), and Maldonado-Torres (2007, 2016), threading together theories of disidentification, 'feeling brown', coloniality, intersectionality, the de-/anti-/post-colonial and critical psychology to develop a 'queerly raced' phenomenological interpretative framework. I have utilised Black feminist and de-/anti-/post-colonial theory, which have often been marginalised within critical and mainstream psychologies despite providing rich possibilities for addressing the social, political, and historical contexts of racialisation and subjectification as well as their intersubjective, subjective, and psychic dimensions.

This work has been a disruption and intervention into British critical and traditional psychologies, challenging 'disciplinary decadence' and our disciplines to no longer ignore coloniality and race as foundational and engage beyond our disciplinary boundaries (Gordon, 2014, p. 81). I join a continuum of scholars and scholarship who have worked and continue to work for a psychology that can understand and challenge coloniality and how it shapes both the colonised and the coloniser, a psychology that can grapple with the specificities of our historical location and no longer desire pallid ahistorical universalisms.

In this book I have centred the experiences of queer and trans people of colour, borne of the frustrations of having been taught a psychology that colluded with the British 'commitment to racelessness' and forms of 'silent racialisations' (Goldberg, 2009, p. 93; El-Tayeb, 2011, p. xx). In centring coloniality and typically marginalised scholarship within UK psychology, such as that of Fanon and others, I have argued for an exploration of the experiences of Black and brown people. Psychology must attend to interlocking power relations and how they shape and affect our material and subjective lives. Subjectivity is marked by the violence of these power relations, and as Nayak (2015, p. 53) notes, 'racist, homophobic, [transphobic], patriarchal, subordinating power structures that appear as external get under the skin, into the psyche' constituting our subjective and material lives in myriad ways.

British psychology has not attended to the rich inner life-worlds and material realities of Black and brown people, almost as if we do not have inner worlds, instead focusing on the ways in which we are pathological and a problem. In this current moment there is momentum for an attention to our (inner) life-worlds, how they are shaped by coloniality and the possibilities of naming these, this disorientation, and their potentialities for liberatory movements. What are the possibilities that disorientation holds for collective action (Ahmed, 2006)? I hope this is an example of a critical psychology in which Black Lives Matter, of the possibilities of a radical, disruptive, Black feminist, queer, intersectional critical psychology that can attend to the structural, to coloniality in the British context, and how it shapes and constrains the possibilities of our lives and how we can and do resist, work on, and against these.

Methodology

In employing this rich theoretical work, I developed a queerly raced phenomenological analytical framework to analyse the feeling and embodied lived experience of being-in-the-world for queer and trans people of colour. Unlike other forms of phenomenology, in utilising Ahmed (2006) and Fanon's (1986) interventions, this framework maintains an attention to the macro-social structures and the political, social, and historical contexts which shape QTPOC subjectivities and possibilities for being in the world.

Following Fanon (1986, p. 111), there cannot be a phenomenology that can simply attend to bodily experience in the world without acknowledging the 'historico-racial schema' through which Black and brown people have been 'woven' out of a 'thousand details, anecdotes and stories'. Meaning is imposed on Black and brown people through the processes of racialisation particular to the British post-colonial context, and this cannot be dismissed in a phenomenological exploration. Building on Fanon, Ahmed (2006) queers phenomenology by exploring how we are orientated towards and around white heteronormativity and how for those of us who cannot follow these lines we experience a form of disorientation. Utilising intersectionality, the queerly raced phenomenological analysis has provided a framework to consider the experience of the intersections of being multiply minoritised through the intersections of race, gender, and sexuality through the lens of coloniality. This has enabled an exploration of how subjectivity is shaped and the possibilities of the intersections, the borderlands, and the fracture. Following Ahmed (2006) I consider the collective potentialities of the experience of disorientation, that by coming together and sharing this angle of vision queer and trans people of colour create possibilities for their own liberation.

The methodology was developed through what Nayak (2015, p. 33) described as a form of Black feminist methodology – a refusal of objectifying objectivity and a move towards 'feeling one's way' in research. This was a welcoming of subjectivity, of the uses of the erotic in being open to others and my own experience, that 'feeling one's way' is part of the

> dialogical relationship between experience, practice and scholarship [that] produces the methodology of the activism of Black feminist theory, where the how to do, and the doing, of the project intersect.
>
> *(p. 33)*

Drawing on this and threading together with Johnson's (2015, p. 157) use of the queer 'reparative ethic' I developed a Black queer feminist epistemological and ontological orientation to the research. This was part of a decolonial impulse to challenge and reject the ways of scholarship which dehumanise the researcher and researched, as if they are separate entities, and as a 'counter-practice' which values human inter-connection, love, and care (Maldonado-Torres, 2016, p. 10). This was also an understanding of analysis as an intimate dialogical encounter, an openness to an understanding of being and subjectivity as always on the way – in process, not fixed, welcoming the 'unavailability of a unified solution' (Nayak, 2015, p. 100).

Possibilities for intersectional richness

Belonging

This book has highlighted the question of belonging for queer and trans people of colour. The commitment to racelessness in the UK alongside the coding of queerness and transness in whiteness left participants unintelligible and fragmented, disorientated in their 'failure' to orientate around and towards white hetero-/homonormativity. This melancholic experience could be understood as a condition of coloniality, as a form of 'racial melancholia' in which queer and trans people of colour are haunted by the losses of our histories, of the possibility of belonging, and of the psycho-existential difficulties of being when being is defined by and through whiteness.

Building community

Following Munoz (2007), QTPOC activism provides the possibilities of 'feeling together in difference'; of the potential productive potentialities of racial melancholia, of 'feeling brown' or, as I name it, feeling 'queerly raced' together. It is through this feeling together that participants could understand the melancholic and disturbing, depressive feelings of not belonging and understand their own negation. It is through collectivism that participants could unearth coloniality as shaping psycho-existentialist problems – as experiencing oneself as a problem as a product of white supremacy and coloniality. There is the possibility of 'owning the negation ... owning an understanding of self and group as a problem in relation to a dominant order, a normative national affect' (Munoz, 2007, p. 445). Using Munoz's work, we can understand that the shared 'nausea' of 'negation' as queerly raced subjects is collectivised and transmitted through intra- and inter-racial 'emphatic projective identification' in which QTPOC belong together in difference (Ahmed, 2006, p. 139; Munoz, 2007, p. 445). Through this collectivism and activism there was a raising of critical, decolonising consciousness. There is an understanding of the self as negated through the processes of intersecting multiple minoritisations, and drawing on histories of non-belonging, feeling queerly raced for QTPOC can be theorised as a 'shared and historicized affective particularity' (Munoz, 2007, p. 450). Through QTPOC activism there is the possibility of collectivism and solidarity as the salve, the balm to both utilise and work on the racially melancholic and depressive 'queerly raced' feelings as well as resist the internalisation of the self as the problem, together.

In feeling together through difference QTPOC shared the importance of and their commitment to authentic connection with one another, of the 'life-affirming' (Sasha) nature of embodied recognition and of being 'deeply invested' (Kai) in one another. In feeling queerly raced together there was an understanding of feeling outside normative modes of belonging, of feeling loss and grief of histories of colonialism, slavery, and losses of the complexities and nuances of sexual and gender expression within cultures of origin. Feeling queerly raced together enabled a recognition of each other and the creation of spaces of belonging premised on shared experiences of non-belonging. The joy and eroticism of recognition and the sharing of feeling queerly raced speak to the sensuality of bodies in struggle together and underline these experiences as affective and passionate. This provides possibilities for new forms of subjectivity and identity, creating spaces of resistance to and dis-identification from white heteronormativity and a reclamation of the potentialities for expansive, decolonising, Black, brown, and 'of colour' queerness and transness.

Decolonising gender and sexuality

QTPOC spaces provided participants with the opportunity to develop rich and more nuanced understandings of the intersections of race, gender, and sexuality. This challenged the typical fragmentary discourses of Blackness and brownness as separate from queerness and transness and of basic understandings of ingrained, essentialist 'Black' or 'brown' homophobia. QTPOC spaces offered participants the possibilities to complicate and de-colonise gender and sexuality.

Participants shared the processes of unearthing painful histories of white supremacy and coloniality – making sense of how Black and brown people's very being are constructed as pathological and other and how this extended through all aspects of their subjectivities including sexuality and gender regardless of orientation. Sasha's experience of feeling together through difference with other queer and trans people of colour allowed her to make room to extend her understandings through her work with young people. She began to complicate her understanding of homophobia within Black communities and the defensive mechanism of the performance of homophobia from young Black men she worked with. Sasha was able to understand the effects of racialised and classed stereotypes in shaping and constraining the young Black men's subjectivities through being open to being in dialogue with them and feeling together in difference (Fanon, 1986).

Similarly, Ashok/a, in being in community with other trans people of colour, began to understand the limitations of trans narratives as relating to white normativity. Through feeling together in difference with other trans people of colour they were able to complicate trans narratives through racialisation, state violence, and coloniality to make sense of their own lived experience and subjectivity. Both Sasha and Ashok/a were able to develop a decolonising queer politic which began to understand cis-heteronormativity as racialised. They began to develop theory, practice, and embodied knowledge as to how queerphobia and transphobia and queerness and transness have differing and complex manifestations and embodiments when understood in the context of slavery, colonialism,

Conclusion 117

and coloniality. This enabled Ashok/a to have a more open dialogue and understanding with their parents about their gender – that working through their 'cis programming' was 'utterly intertwined' with their decolonising politics.

Through QTPOC spaces participants were able to develop a decolonising queer politic. This provided the potential for deeper, richer understandings of coloniality, making space to excavate the 'profound wounds' of coloniality (Maldonado-Torres, 2007, p. 24). Participants shared a deep commitment to QTPOC and wider Black and brown communities, grappling with and making space for new understandings of the complexities of coloniality and liberation. These decolonising queer politics, to paraphrase Fanon, showed a belief in the radical possibilities of decolonial love; as Sandoval (2000, p. 158) notes it is 'love that can access and guide our theoretical and political "movidas" – revolutionary maneuvers toward decolonized being' (Fanon, 2007, p. 181). QTPOC could be understood as what Anzaldua (2009, p. 43) described as *nepantlera*, bridges who span 'liminal (threshold) spaces between worlds'. Bridging is 'the work of opening the gate to the stranger, within and without', an attempt to build community, and for which 'we must risk being open to personal, political and spiritual intimacy, to risk being wounded' (p. 246). In understanding QTPOC as *nepantlera* we can understand bridging 'as an act of will, an act of [decolonial] love, an attempt toward compassion and reconciliation, and a promise to be present with the pain of others without losing themselves to it' (p. 246). QTPOC were willing to be present with and address the 'profound wounds' of coloniality even as they risked being wounded (Maldonado-Torres, 2007, p. 24). Participants moved towards the difficult and painful issues that shaped their own isolation and fragmentation in order to develop richer, more nuanced understandings, and I argue, that this was motivated by decolonial love for self and community and a desire to be in dialogue with each other.

Participants shared the development of an intersectional, decolonising understanding of the racialised, gendered, and sexual pathologisation of all Black and brown people and how this could and was operationalised against each other. Sasha and Ashok/a's examples of bridging attempted to build understanding and community and could be understood as exploring the potential solidarities between heterosexual and cisgender and queer and trans Black and brown folks. I therefore suggest, following Cohen (2004, p. 28), that we should explore what it may look like to centre 'deviance' in resistance to coloniality – if wider movements for Black and brown liberation struggles rejected respectability politics that harm all but particularly those most minoritised such as queer and trans folks, and, for example, those outside of the heteronormative family structure, those in poverty, those in sex work. This would provide decolonial potential for challenging hegemonic discourse and politics that continue to centre colonial constructions of Blackness and brownness as pathological; creating possibilities for centring those most minoritised; and building 'counter-normative space' expanding what and who is queer (Cohen, 2004; Maldonado-Torres, 2016, p. 38).

We can understand these moves to decolonising queer politic, motivated by deep commitment and decolonial love for each other, as within a continuum of Black, of colour, and Caribbean feminist and queer and trans work which illuminates the ways in which race, gender, and sexuality co-construct one another as part of the ongoing project of coloniality (for example, see Hammonds, 1994; Spillers, 2003; Cohen, 2004; Alexander, 2005; Lugones, 2007, 2010; Snorton, 2017; Tinsley, 2019; Leo, 2020). Future work may want to further explore these connections and foster further dialogue and solidarities.

Conflict and harm in community: the possibilities for the reparative and transformative

The development of a decolonising queer politic, and the generous approach to the other when dealing with the 'profound wounds' of coloniality are, I suggest, a reparative act drawing on wider movements for transformative justice and community accountability. Participants shared an investment in transformative approaches and concerns around 'replicating punitive and carceral logics, which are inherently racist, classist, homophobic, transphobic and misogynist' and sought to make conflicts 'generative' to transform individuals, relationships, and the 'culture and power dynamics of the community' (Bonsu, 2020, p. 35).

Participants grappled with how to manage conflict and harm within QTPOC communities, beyond punitive approaches and this was something that throughout the research period was echoed within wider queer discourse and communities. These issues are also complicated by what Sedgwick (2003, p. 682) described as the privileging of paranoid critique – that a paranoid reading of each other has 'become routine rather than critical thinking', and that this is borne out of an obsession with the 'unveiling of an external threat'. This permeates queer communities, through which 'our relational potentiality is diminished' (p. 683). Participants shared how paranoid readings could sometimes cause difficulties within QTPOC spaces, particularly in relation to conflict. This raises questions of what it may mean to come together through shared experiences of negation, trauma, injury, and harm; how this can shape spaces for those who are multiply minoritised; and acknowledging that when experiencing oppression paranoid readings are of use but cannot inform the ways in which we build communities and move towards liberation.

Following Munoz (2006, p. 675; 2007, p. 444), I suggest a way of resisting paranoid readings of each other is to emphasise an ethical position which taps into what he describes as 'feeling brown, feeling down' together, of 'feeling together in difference'. This is an 'affective particularity' of feeling together in difference, building on the productive potential of racial melancholia and feeling queerly raced (Munoz, 2006, p. 676). This goes beyond identity to what it is like to feel together as 'minoritarian subjects' (p. 676). This provides possibilities for the collective and a potential ethics for relating to one another, resisting the paranoid–schizoid position, and moving towards a depressive position which can be reparative. This provides possibilities for generative conflict and collective struggle, centring a politics of decolonial love – drawing from the erotics of feeling together in difference. Through focusing on the sociality of feeling queerly raced, together, the individual and the collective can resist the foreclosure of a reparative and hopeful politics. It is clear from participants' erotic experiences of connection and joy within QTPOC activism that there are possibilities for the reparative; however, the potentialities of feeling queerly raced together may sometimes be under-utilised.

Future praxis and research may want to explore ways in which the erotics of feeling together in difference can be nurtured and utilised; consider the ways in which trauma and oppression shape the culture of activist movements and generously challenge them; and continue to develop transformative approaches to conflict to strengthen QTPOC communities and activism.

Possibilities for intersectional richness

I suggest QTPOC groups are spaces for possibilities for reclaiming our intersectional richness. These are spaces in which fragmented understandings of subjectivity; race, gender, sexuality; historical, social, and political contexts; and modernity/coloniality are challenged. These provide possibilities for understanding the richness of intersectionality and refuse pallid, universal, ahistorical, and colonial constructions of human experience and subjectivities. This opens potentialities for new forms of subjectivities and the freedom of understanding subjectivity and being as 'always on the way'. A decolonising queer politic makes possibilities for expansiveness, plentifulness, and interconnection through feeling together in difference, resisting the ways that coloniality and white cis-heteronormativity attempt to drain away the fullness of our lives. Through feeling 'queerly raced', feeling through difference together, community and resistance to coloniality and fragmentation can be strengthened. In emphasising connection, the reparative, and the erotic this capacity can be further developed.

REFERENCES

Ahmed, S. (2006). *Queer Phenomenology: Orientations, Objects, Others*. Durham: Duke University Press.
Akerlund, M. and Cheung, M. (2000). Teaching Beyond the Deficit Model: Gay and Lesbian Issues among African Americans, Latinos, and Asian Americans. *Journal of Social Work and Education, 36*, 2.
Alexander, M.J. (2005). *Pedagogies of Crossing. Meditations on Feminism, Sexual Politics, Memory, and the Sacred*. Durham and London: Duke University Press.
Alldred, P. and Fox, N. (2015). From 'Lesbian and Gay Psychology' to a Critical Psychology of Sexualities. In I. Parker (Ed.), *Handbook of Critical Psychology* (pp. 200–210). East Sussex: Routledge.
Annells, M. (1996). Hermeneutic Phenomenology: Philosophical Perspectives and Current Use in Nursing Research. *Journal of Advanced Nursing, 23*, 705–713.
Anzaldua, G. (1987). *Borderlands/La Frontera: The New Mestiza*. San Francisco: Aunt Lute Books.
Anzaldua, G. (2009). (Un)natural Bridges, (Un)safe Spaces. In A.L. Keating (Ed.), *The Gloria Anzaldúa Reader* (pp. 243–248). Durham: Duke University Press.
Aspden, K. (2008). *The Hounding of David Oluwale*. UK: Vintage.
Balsam, K.F., Molina, Y., Beadnell, B., Simoni, J., and Walters, K. (2011). Measuring Multiple Minority Stress: The LGBT People of Colour Microaggressions Scale. *Cultural Diversity and Ethnic Minority Psychology, 17*, 163–174.
Bell, V. (1999). On Speech, Race and Melancholia: An Interview with Judith Butler. In V. Bell (Ed.), *Performativity and Belonging* (pp. 163–174). London: Sage Publications Limited.
Bhabha, H. (2012). *The Location of Culture*. London: Routledge.
Blackman, L. (2002). A Psychophysics of the Imagination. In V. Walkerdine (Ed.), *Challenging Subjects: Critical Psychology for a New Millennium* (pp. 133–148). New York: Palgrave Macmillan.
Blackman, L., Cromby, J., Hook, D., Papadopoulos, D., and Walkerdine, V. (2008). Creating Subjectivities. *Subjectivity, 22*, 1–27.
Bonsu, J.E. (2020). Excerpt from "Black Queer Feminism as Praxis: Building an Organization and a Movement". In E. Dixon and L. Lakshmi Piepzna-Samarasinha

(Eds.), *Beyond Survival: Strategies and Stories from the Transformative Justice Movement* (pp. 35–38). California: AK Press.
Brah, A. (1996). *Cartographies of Diaspora: Contesting Identities.* London and New York: Routledge.
Brah, A. and Phoenix, A. (2004). Ain't I a Woman? Revisiting Intersectionality. *Journal of International Women's Studies,* 5, 75–86.
Brown, W. (1995). *States of Injury: Power and Freedom in Late Modernity.* West Sussex: Princeton University Press.
Brown, S. and Stenner, P. (2009). *Psychology without Foundations: History, Philosophy and Psychosocial Theory.* London: Sage.
Browne, K., Banerjea, N., McGlynn, N., Bakshi, L., Beethi, S., and Biswas, R. (2021). The Limits of Legislative Change: Moving beyond Inclusion/Exclusion to Create 'A Life Worth Living'. *Environment and Planning C: Politics and Space,* 39, 31–52.
Boyce Davies, C. (2008). *Left of Karl Marx: The Political Life of Black Communist Claudia Jones.* Durham and London: Duke University Press.
Browne, K. and Nash, C. (2014). Resisting LGBT Rights Where "We Have Won": Canada and Great Britain. *Journal of Human Rights,* 13, 322–336.
Burr, V. (1999). *Social Constructionism* (2nd ed.). London and New York: Routledge.
Butler, J. (1997). *Theories in Subjection: The Psychic Life of Power.* Stanford: Stanford University Press.
Capdevila, R. and Lazard, L. (2015). Psychology of Women. Questions of Politics and Practice. In I. Parker (Ed.) *Handbook of Critical Psychology* (pp. 191–199). East Sussex: Routledge.
Carmen, Gail, Shaila, and Pratibha. (1984). Becoming Visible: Black Lesbian Discussions. *Feminist Review,* 17, 1, 53–72. https://warwick.ac.uk/fac/arts/history/research/centres/blackstudies/carmen._gail._shalia._pratibha._becoming_visible.pdf
Cheng, A.A. (1997). The Melancholy of Race. *The Kenyon Review,* 19, 49–61.
Cheng Thom, K. (2019). *I Hope We Choose Love: A Trans Girl's Notes from the End of the World.* Canada: Arsenal Pulp Press.
Chowdhury, T. (2019). Policing the 'Black Party' – Racialised Drugs Policing at Festivals in the UK. In K. Koram (Ed.), *The War on Drugs and the Global Colour Line* (pp. x-x). London: Pluto Press.
Clemon, G., Adam, B.D., Read, S.E., Husbands, W.C., Remis, R.S., Mahoroka, L., and Bourke, S.B. (2012). The MaBwana Black Men's Study: Community and Belonging in the Lives of African, Caribbean and Other Black Gay Men in Toronto. *Culture, Health and Sexuality,* 14, 5, 549–562.
Cohen, C.J. (2004). Deviance as Resistance: A New Research Agenda for the Study of Black Politics. *DuBois Review,* 1, 27–45.
Colpani, G. and Habed, A.J. (2014). "In Europe It's Different": Homonationalism and Peripheral Desires for Europe. In P.M. Ayoub and D. Paternotte (Eds.), *LGBT Activism and the Making of Europe: A Rainbow Europe?* (pp. 73–97). UK: Palgrave Macmillan.
The Combahee River Collective. (1977). *The Combahee River Collective Statement.* Retrieved 11 August 2020 from https://www.blackpast.org/african-american-history/combahee-river-collective-statement-1977/.
Craib, I. (2001). *Psychoanalysis: A Critical Introduction.* Cambridge: Polity Press.
Crenshaw, K. (1989). Demarginalizing the Intersection of Race and Sex: A Black Feminist Critique of Anti-Discrimination Doctrine, Feminist Theory and Anti-Racist Politics. *University of Chicago Legal Forum,* 1, 139–167.
Crenshaw, K. (1992). Whose Story Is It, Anyway? Feminist and Anti-Racist Appropriations of Anita Hill. In T. Morrison (Ed.), *Race-ing Justice, En-gendering Power: Essays on Anita*

Hill, Clarence Thomas and the Construction of Social Reality (pp. 402–440). New York: Pantheon Books.

Crenshaw, K. (2016). *On Intersectionality. Key Note Speech at Women of the World Festival 2016*. Retrieved 14 December 2021 from https://www.youtube.com/watch?v=-DW4HLgYPlA.

Cvetkovich, A. (2012). Depression Is Ordinary: Public Feelings and Sadiya Hartman's Lose Your Mother. *Feminist Theory, 13*, 131–146.

Cvetkovich, A. (2014). Turning into the Sense of Brown. *Boundary 2*. Retrieved 6 January 2021 from http://boundary2.org/2014/03/10/turning-in-to-the-sense-of-brown/.

Cyrus, K. (2017). Multiple Minorities as Multiply Marginalized: Applying the Minority Stress Theory to LGBTQ People of Colour. *Journal of Gay and Lesbian Mental Health, 21*, 3, 194–202.

Desai, M.U. (2014). Psychology, the Psychological, and Critical Praxis: A Phenomenologist Reads Frantz Fanon. *Theory & Psychology, 24*, 58–75.

Dhamoon, R.K. (2011). Considerations on Mainstreaming Intersectionality. *Political Research Quarterly, 64*, 230–243.

Dixon, E. (2020). Building Community Safety: Practical Steps toward Liberatory Transformation. In E. Dixon and L. Lakshmi Piepzna-Samarasinha (Eds.), *Beyond Survival: Strategies and Stories from the Transformative Justice Movement* (pp. 11–18). California: AK Press.

Dominguez, M.L. (2017). LGBTQIA People of Color: Utilizing the Cultural Psychology Model as a Guide for the Mental Health Assessment and Treatment of Patients with Diverse Identities. *Journal of Gay and Lesbian Mental Health, 21*, 3, 203–220.

Douglas, S., Jivraj, S., and Lamble, S. (2011). Liabilities of Queer Anti-Racist Critique. *Feminist Legal Studies, 19*, 2, 107–118.

DuBois, W.E.B. (2016). *The Souls of Black Folk*. New York: Dover Publications.

Durazo, A.C.R., Bierria, A., and Kim, M. (2012). Community Accountability: Emerging Movements to Transform Violence. *Social Justice: A Journal of Crime, Conflict and World Order, 37*, 4. Retrieved 7 January 2021 from https://communityaccountability.wordpress.com/social-justice-journal-issue/.

Elin Fisher, S.D. (2016). Pauli Murray's Peter Panic. Perspectives from the Margins of Gender and Race in Jim Crow America. *TSQ: Transgender Studies Quarterly, 3*, 95–103.

El-Tayeb, F. (2011). *European Others: Queering Ethnicity in Postnational Europe*. Minnesota: University of Minnesota Press.

El-Tayeb, F. (2012). 'Gays Who Cannot Be Properly Gay': Queer Muslims in the Neoliberal European City. *European Journal of Women's Studies, 19*, 79–95.

Eng, D.L. and Han, S. (2000). A Dialogue on Racial Melancholia. *Psychoanalytic Dialogues, 10*, 667–700.

Fanon, F. (1986). *Black Skins, White Masks*. London: Pluto Press.

Fanon, F. (2007). *Black Skins, White Masks*. London: Pluto Press.

Fanon, F. (2008). *Black Skins, White Masks*. London: Penguin Classics.

Fatsis, L. (2019). Grime: Criminal Subculture Or Public Counterculture? A Critical Investigation into the Criminalization of Black Musical Subcultures in the UK. *Crime, Media, Culture, 15*, 3, 447–461.

Ferguson, R.A. (2004). *Aberrations in Black: Toward a Queer of Colour Critique*. Minneapolis: University of Minnesota Press.

Finlay, L. (2009). Debating Phenomenological Research Methods. *Phenomenology and Practice, 3*, 6–25.

Garvey, C.J., Mobley Jr, S.D., Summerville, K.S., and Moore, G.T. (2019). Queer and Trans* Students of Color: Navigating Identity Disclosure and College Contexts. *The Journal of Higher Education, 90*, 1, 150–178.

Gilles, V., Harden, A., Johnson, K., Reavey, P., Strange, V. and Willig, C. (2005). Painting Pictures of Embodied Experience: The Use of NonVerbal Data Production for the Study of Embodiment. *Qualitative Research in Psychology, 2*, 199–212.

Gilroy, P. (2013). *There Ain't No Black in the Union Jack*. London: Routledge Classics.

Giwa, S. and Greensmith, C. (2012). Race Relations and Racism in the LGBTQ Community of Toronto: Perceptions of Gay and Queer Service Providers of Color. *Journal of Homosexuality, 59*, 2, 149–185.

Golash-Boza, T. (2016). A Critical and Comprehensive Sociological Theory of Race and Racism. *Sociology of Race and Ethnicity, 2*, 129–141.

Goldberg, D.T. (2009). *The Threat of Race: Reflections on Racial Neoliberalism*. Oxford: Wiley-Blackwell.

Gordon, L.R. (2014). Disciplinary Decadence and the Decolonisation of Knowledge. *Africa Development, XXXIX*, 81–92.

Gough, B. (2015). Qualitative Methods: Critical Practices and Prospects from a Diverse Field. In I. Parker (Ed.), *Handbook of Critical Psychology* (pp. 107–116). East Sussex: Routledge.

Hall, J.M. (2012). Revalorized Black Embodiment: Dancing with Fanon. *Journal of Black Studies, 43*, 274–288.

Hall, S. (1978). *Policing the Crisis: Mugging, the State, and Law and Order*. London: Macmillan.

Hagai, E.B., Annechino, R., Young, N., and Antin, T. (2020). Intersecting Sexual Identities, Oppressions, and Social Justice Work: Comparing LGBTQ Baby Boomers to Millennials Who Came of Age after the 1980s AIDS Epidemic. *Journal of Social Issues, 776*, 971–992.

Hailey, J., Burton, W., and Arscott, J. (2020). We are Family: Chosen and Created Families as a Protective Factor against Racialised Trauma and Anti-LGBTQ Oppression among African American Sexual and Gender Minority Youth. *Journal of GLBT Family Studies, 16*, 2, 176–191.

Hammonds, E. (1994). Black (W)holes and the Geometry of Black Female Sexuality. *Differences: A Journal of Feminist Cultural Studies, 6*, 2–3, 126.

Haraway, D. (1988). Situated Knowledges: The Science Question in Feminism and the Privilege of Partial Perspective. *Feminist Studies, 14*, 3, 575–599.

Haritaworn, J. (2015). *Queer Lovers and Hateful Others; Regenerating Violent Times and Places*. London: Pluto Press.

Hartman, S. (2006). *Lose Your Mother: A Journey along the Atlantic Slave Route*. New York: Farrar Straus Giroux.

Hartman, S. (2019). *Wayward Lives, Beautiful Experiments: Intimate Histories of Riotous Black Girls, Troublesome Women and Queer Radicals*. London: Profile Books.

Heath, C. (2009, 1 April). De Menezes: The Real Story. *The Independent*. Retrieved 6 January 2021 from https://www.independent.co.uk/news/uk/crime/de-menezes-the-real-story-6095269.html.

Henriques, J., Hollway, W., Urwin, C., Venn, C., and Walkerdine, V. (1984). *Changing the Subject: Psychology, Social Regulation and Subjectivity*. London and New York: Routledge.

Hesse, B. (2000). Diasporicity: Black Britain's Post-Colonial Formations. In B. Hesse (Ed.), *Un/Settled Multiculturalisms: Diasporas, Entanglements, 'Transruptions'* (pp. 96–120). London: Zed Books.

Hesse, B. (2004). Im/Plausible Deniability: Racism's Conceptual Double Bind. *Social Identities*, 10, 9–29.
Hesse, B. and Sayyid, S. (2002). The 'War' against Terrorism/The 'War' for Cynical Reason. *Ethnicities*, 2, 149–154.
Hill Collins, P. and Bilge, S. (2020). *Intersectionality* (2nd ed.). Cambridge: Polity Press.
Hines, S. (2019). The Feminist Frontier: On Trans and Feminism. *Journal of Gender Studies*, 28, 2, 145–157.
Hook, D. (2008). The 'Real' of Racializing Embodiment. *Journal of Community and Applied Social Psychology*, 18, 2, 140–152.
Human Rights Watch. (2008). *This Alien Legacy: The Origins of "Sodomy" Laws in British Colonialism*. Retrieved 6 January 2021 from https://www.hrw.org/report/2008/12/17/alien-legacy/origins-sodomy-laws-british-colonialism.
Hunt, S. and Holmes, C. (2015). Everyday Decolonization: Living a Decolonizing Queer Politics. *Journal of Lesbian Studies*, 19, 154–172.
Hunter, M.A. (2010). All the Gays Are White and all the Blacks Are Straight: Black Gay Men, Identity, and Community. *Sex Research and Social Policy*, 7, 81–92.
Johnson, K. (2015). *Sexuality: A Psychosocial Manifesto*. Cambridge: Polity Press.
Jones, L. (2016). "If a Muslim Says 'Homo', Nothing Gets Done": Racist Discourse and In-group Identity Construction in an LGBT Youth Group. *Language in Society*, 45, 113–133.
Josephides, S. (1991). Towards a History of the Indian Workers' Association. *Research Paper in Ethnic Relations*, 18, 1–57.
Kim, M. (2012). Moving Beyond Critique: Creative Interventions and Reconstructions of Community Accountability. *Social Justice: A Journal of Crime, Conflict and World Order*, 37, 14–35. Retrieved 7 January 2021 from https://communityaccountability.wordpress.com/social-justice-journal-issue/.
Kim, U. (1999). After the 'Crisis' in Social Psychology: The Development of the Transactional Model of Science. *Asian Journal of Social Psychology*, 2, 1–9.
Kristeva, J. (1980). Oscillation between Power and Denial. In E. Marks and I. de Courtivron (Eds.), *New French Feminisms: An Anthology* (pp. 165–167). Amherst: The University of Massachusetts Press.
Kulick, A., Wernick, L.J., Woodford, M.R., and Renn, K. (2017). Heterosexism, Depression, and Campus Engagement among LGBTQ College Students: Intersectional Differences and Opportunities for Healing. *Journal of Homosexuality*, 64, 8, 1125–1141.
Lawrence, M. and Taylor, Y. (2020). The UK Government LGBT Action Plan: Discourses of Progress, Enduring Stasis, and LGBTQI+ Lives 'Getting Better'. *Critical Social Policy*, 40, 586–607.
Leo, B. (2020). The Colonial/Modern [Cis]Gender System and Trans World Traveling. *Hypatia*, 35, 454–474.
Lewis, G. (2000). *'Race', Gender, Social Welfare: Encounters in a Postcolonial Society*. Cambridge: Polity Press.
Lorde, A. (1984). *Sister Outsider: Essays and Speeches*. Berkley, CA: Crossing Press.
Lugones, M. (2007). Heterosexualism and the Colonial/Modern Gender System. *Hypatia*, 1, 186–209.
Lugones, M. (2010). Towards a Decolonial Feminism. *Hypatia*, 25, 742–759.
Maldonado-Torres, N. (2007). On the Coloniality of Being. *Cultural Studies*, 21, 2–3.
Maldonado-Torres, N. (2016). *Outline of Ten Theses on Coloniality and Decoloniality*. Foundation Frantz Fanon. Retrieved from http://fondation-frantzfanon.com/outline-of-ten-theses-on-coloniality-and-decoloniality/ [last accessed December 14, 2021].

Mama, A. (1995). *Beyond the Masks: Race, Gender and Subjectivity*. London: Routledge.
Mason-John, V. (1995). *Talking Black: Lesbians of African and Asian Descent Speak Out*. London: Cassell.
Mason-John, V. and Khambatta, A. (1993). *Lesbians Talk: Making Black Waves*. London: Scarlet Press.
Mattos, A. (2015). Feminist Psychology. Researches, Interventions, Challenges. In I. Parker (Ed.), *Handbook of Critical Psychology* (pp. 329–338). East Sussex: Routledge.
Mehmood, T.A. (2008). Marginalisation, Resistance and the Road to Fictional Visibility. *South Asian Cultural Studies*, 4, 1, 3–11.
Meyer, D. (2012). An Intersectional Analysis of Lesbian, Gay, Bisexual, and Transgender (LGBT) People's Evaluations of Anti-Queer Violence. *Gender and Society*, 26, 6, 849–873.
Meyer, I.H. (2003). Prejudice, Social Stress, and Mental Health in Lesbian, Gay, and Bisexual Populations: Conceptual Issues and Research Evidence. *Psychological Bulletin*, 129, 5, 674–697.
Meyer, I.H. (2010). Identity, Stress, and Resilience in Lesbians, Gay Men and Bisexuals of Colour. *The Counseling Psychologist*, 38, 3, 442–454.
Millet, G.A., Jeffries, W.L., Peterson, J.L., Malebranche, D.J., Lane, T., Flores, S.A., Fenton, K.A., Wilson, P.A., Steiner, R. and Heilig, C.M. (2012). Common Roots: A Contextual Review of HIV Epidemics in Black Men Who Have Sex with Men across the African Diaspora. *Lancet*, 380, 411–423.
Mirza, H.S. (Ed.) (1997). *Black British Feminism: A Reader*. London: Routledge.
Moore, D.L. (2012). Using the Erotic to Do Our Work. *Paper presented at The Kennedy School, Harvard University as part of the Audre Lorde Human Rights Lecture Series*. Retrieved 6 January 2021 from http://www.thefeministwire.com/2014/02/using-erotic-work/.
Munoz, J.E. (1999). *Disidentifications: Queers of Color and the Performance of Politics*. Minneapolis: University of Minnesota Press.
Munoz, J.E. (2006). Feeling Brown, Feeling Down: Latina Affect, the Performativity of Race, and the Depressive Position. *Signs*, 31, 675–688.
Munoz, J.E. (2007). "Chico, What Does It Feel Like to Be a Problem?" The Transmission of Brownness. In J. Flores and R. Rosaldo (Eds.), *A Companion to Latina/o Studies* (pp. 441–451). Oxford: Blackwell Publishing.
Nayak, S. (2015). *Race, Gender, and the Activism of Black Feminist Theory: Working with Audre Lorde*. New York: Routledge.
Nguyen, J. and Koontz Anthony, A. (2014). Black Authenticity: Defining the Ideals and Expectations in the Construction of "Real" Blackness. *Sociology Compass*, 8, 770–778.
Papadopoulos, D. (2008). In the Ruins of Representation: Identity, Individuality, Subjectification. *British Journal of Social Psychology*, 47, 139–165.
Parker, I. (2015). *Handbook of Critical Psychology*. East Sussex: Routledge.
Pastrana, J.A. (2010). Privileging Oppression: Contradictions in Intersectional Politics. *Western Journal of Black Studies*, 34, 1, 53–60.
Pearce, R., Erikainen, S., and Vincent, B. (2020). TERF Wars: An Introduction. *The Sociological Review Monographs*, 68, 4, 677–698.
Penaloza, M.R. and Ubach, T.C. (2015). Queer Theory: Disarticulating Critical Psychology. In I. Parker (Ed.), *Handbook of Critical Psychology* (pp. 339–347). East Sussex: Routledge.
Perez, R. (2012). *Mark Aguhar's Critical Flippancy*. Bully Bloggers. Retrieved 6 January 2021 from https://bullybloggers.wordpress.com/2012/08/04/mark-aguhars-critical-flippancy/.

Phoenix, A. (2013). Decolonising Practices: Negotiating Narratives from Racialised and Gendered Experiences of Education. In H.S. Mirza and C. Joseph (Eds.), *Black and Postcolonial Feminisms in New Times: Researching Educational Inequalities* (pp. 101–114). London: Routledge.

Phoenix, A. and Pattynama, P. (2006). Intersectionality. *European Journal of Women's Studies, 13*, 187–192.

Pierce, C.M. (1974). Psychiatric Problems of the Black Minority. In S. Arieti (Ed.), *American Handbook of Psychiatry* (pp. 512–523). New York: Basic Books. Retrieved 13 September 2021 from https://www.freepsychotherapybooks.org/ebook/psychiatric-problems-of-the-black-minority/.

Puar, J.K. (2008, 2 May). Q & A with Jasbir Puar. *Dark Matter (3)*. Retrieved 16 January 2021 from http://www.darkmatter 101.org/site/2008/05/02/qa-with-jasbir-puar/.

Puar, J.K. (2007). *Terrorist Assemblages: Homonationalism in Queer Times*. Durham and London: Duke University Press.

Quijano, A. (2007). Coloniality and Modernity/Rationality. *Cultural Studies, 21*, 2–3, 168–178.

Rabaka, R. (2010). *Forms of Fanonism: Frantz Fanon's Critical Theory and The Dialectics of Decolonization*. Maryland: Lexington Books.

Raboin, T. (2017). Exhortations of Happiness: Liberalism and Nationalism in the Discourses on LGBTI Asylum Rights in the UK. *Sexualities, 20*, 5–6, 663–681.

Rage, R. (2016). Recounting and Reflecting on Resistance: The Dilemma of the Diaspora to Define. In S. Bakshi, S. Jivraj and S. Posocco (Eds.), *Decolonising Sexualities: Transnational Perspectives, Critical Interventions* (pp. 47–59). Oxford: Counterpress.

Ramamurthy, A. (2013). *Black Star: Britain's Asian Youth Movements*. London: Pluto Press.

Rassool, N. (1997). Fractured or Flexible Identities? Life Histories of 'Black' Diasporic Women in Britain. In H.S. Mirza (Ed.), *Black British Feminism: A Reader* (pp. 187–204). London: Routledge.

Renault, M. (2011). "Corps a Corps" Frantz Fanon's Erotics of National Liberation. *Journal of French and Francophone Philosophy, 11*, 49–55.

Riggs, D.W. and Augoustinos, M. (2005). The Psychic Life of Colonial Power: Racialised Subjectivities, Bodies and Methods. *Journal of Community and Applied Social Psychology, 15*, 461–477.

Rowe, M. (2008). Micro-Affirmations and Micro-Inequalities. *Journal of the International Ombudsman Association, 1*, 1–9.

Sadika, B., Wiebe, E., Morrison, M.A., and Morrison, T.G. (2020). Intersectional Microaggressions and Social Support for LGBTQ Persons of Color: A Systematic Review of the Canadian-Based Empirical Literature. *Journal of GLBT Family Studies, 16*, 2, 111–147.

Said, E. (1978). *Orientalism*. New York: Pantheon Books.

Sandoval, C. (2000). *Methodology of the Oppressed*. Minneapolis: University of Minnesota Press.

Sayarer, J. (2020, 22 July). Jean Charles De Menezes: 15 years on. *Tribune*. Retrieved 6 January 2021 from https://tribunemag.co.uk/2020/07/jean-charles-de-menezes-15-years-on.

Sedgwick, E.K. (2003). *Touching Feeling: Affect, Pedagogy, Performativity*. Durham and London: Duke University Press.

Sian, K.P. (2015). Spies, Surveillance and Stakeouts: Monitoring Muslim Moves in British State Schools. *Race, Ethnicity and Education, 18*, 2, 183–201.

Sivanandan, A. (1983). Introduction. Challenging Racism: Strategies for the 80s. *Race Class, 25*, 1, 1–11.

Smith, J.A., Flowers, P., and Larkin, M. (2009). *Interpretative Phenomenological Analysis: Theory, Method and Research*. London: Sage Publications Limited.

Smith, H.J. (2013). A Critique of the Teaching Standards in England (1984–2012): Discourses of Equality and Maintaining the Status Quo. *Journal of Education Policy*, 28, 4, 427–448.

Snorton, C.R. (2017). *Black on Both Sides: A Racial History of Trans Identity*. Minneapolis: University of Minnesota Press.

Spillers, H. (2003). *Black, White, and in Color: Essays on American Literature and Culture*. Chicago, IL: University of Chicago Press.

Stonewall. (2012). *One Minority at a Time*. Retrieved 6 January 2021 from https://www.stonewall.org.uk/resources/one-minority-time-2012.

Swaby, N.A. (2014). 'Disparate in Voice, Sympathetic in Direction': Gendered Political Blackness and the Politics of Solidarity. *Feminist Review*, 108, 11–25.

Teo, T. (1999). Methodologies of Critical Psychology: Illustrations from the Field of Racism. *Annual Review of Critical Psychology*, 1, 119–135.

The Latina Feminist Group, 2001. *Telling to Live: Latina Feminist Testimonios*. USA: Duke University Press.

Thomas, P. and Sanderson, P. (2012). Crossing the Line? White Young People and Community Cohesion. *Critical Social Policy*, 33, 1, 160–180.

Tinsley, O.N. (2019). *Ezili's Mirrors: Imagining Black Queer Genders*. Durham: Duke University Press.

Tischner, I. (2013). *Fat Lives: A Feminist Psychological Exploration*. London: Routledge.

Tosh, J. (2015). *Perverse Psychology: The Pathologization of Sexual Violence and Transgenderism*. East Sussex: Routledge.

Traore, C. (2014). Victor Has Not Died! In J.R. Gordon and R. Beadle-Blair (Eds.), *Black and Gay in the UK: An Anthology* (pp. 177–188). London: Team Angelica.

Tudor, A. (2021). Decolonizing Trans/Gender Studies? Teaching Gender, Race, and Sexuality in Times of the Rise of the Global Right. *TSQ: Trans Gender Quarterly*, 8, 238–256.

Ussher, J.M. (2008). Reclaiming Embodiment within Critical Psychology: A Material-Discursive Analysis of the Menopausal Body. *Social And Personality Psychology Compass*, 2, 5, 1781–1798.

Vaccaro, A. and Mena, J.A. (2011). It's Not Burnout, It's More: Queer College Activists of Colour and Mental Health. *Journal of Gay and Lesbian Mental Health*, 15, 339–367.

Venn, C. (2009). Identity, Diasporas and the Subjective Change: The Role of Affect, the Relation to the Other and the Aesthetic. *Subjectivities*, 26, 3–28.

Waite, L. (2012). Neo-assimilationist Citizenship and Belonging Policies in Britain: Meanings for Transnational Migrants in Northern England. *Geoforum*, 43, 353–361.

Walker, J.N.J. and Longmire-Avital, B. (2013). The Impact of Religious Faith and Internalized Homonegativity on Resiliency for Black Lesbian, Gay, and Bisexual Emerging Adults. *Developmental Psychology*, 49, 9, 1723–1731.

Ward, E.G. (2005). Homophobia, Hypermasculinity and the US Black Church. *Culture, Health and Sexuality*, 7, 493–504.

Ward, J. (2008). White Normativity: The Cultural Dimensions of Whiteness in a Racially Diverse LGBT Organisation. *Sociological Perspectives*, 51, 563–586.

Watkins, M. and Shulman, H. (2008). *Toward Psychologies of Liberation*. New York: Palgrave MacMillan.

Wright, M.M. (2013). Can I Call You Black? The Limits of Authentic Heteronormativity in African Diasporic Discourse. *African and Black Diaspora: An International Journal, 6*, 1, 3–16.

Wynter, S. and McKittrick, K. (2015). Unparalleled Catastrophe for Our Species? Or to Give Humanness a Different Future: Conversations. In K. McKittrick (Ed.), *Sylvia Wynter: On Being Human as Praxis* (pp. 9–89). North Carolina: Duke University Press.

Yin, J. (2005). Constructing the Other: A Critical Reading of *The Joy Luck Club*. *The Howard Journal of Communications, 16*, 149–175.

Yuen-Thompson, B. (2012). The Price of 'Community' from Bisexual/Biracial Women's Perspectives. *Journal of Bisexuality, 12*, 417–428.

INDEX

abuse 19, 100, 107–109
activism *see* political organising
affect 32, 40, 41; affective connection 75–77, 84, 115–116, 118–119; affective transmission 83–84, 103, 115; critical psychology 35, 37; feeling brown 83, 110–111, 113, 118; feeling queerly raced 84, 110–111, 115, 118; normative 83, 115
affirmation 76, 80–82; cultural 6; of experience 19, 69–71, 74–75, 78, 80–82, 112; life-affirming 74–75, 115; microaffirmations 75
Ahmed, Sara 18, 24–26, 50–51, 67, 69, 75, 84, 86, 103, 113–115
Alexander, M. Jacqui 94–95, 118
anti-blackness 12, 29, 94
anti-colonialism 5–7, 9, 11, 33–34, 95, 97–98, 113; anti-colonial counter violence 100, 106; heteropatriarchy 95
anti-racist 4, 7, 11, 27, 57
Anzaldua, G. 46, 93, 117
arabic cultures 4, 51–54, 61, 71–72, 88
assimilation 9, 19, 46, 49, 57–59, 61–64, 66, 74, 80, 102–103; ambivalence towards 66–67; loss of whiteness 63–64, 66–67; melancholic experience of 57, 62–64, 66–67
authenticity 2, 12, 17, 23, 58, 64

being-in-the-world 18, 23–26, 28–30, 32, 34, 41, 47, 60, 68, 73, 76, 87, 91, 112, 114

being a problem 22, 50, 61, 67–68, 72–74, 83–84, 113, 115
belonging 19, 22, 27, 62, 115–116; ambivalence about 65–66, 68; being in majority spaces 70; black and brown communities 13, 49; British society 2, 13, 19, 49, 50–53, 56–66; home 67–69, 74–75, 78; impossibility of 64–66; intersectional 49–50, 62, 72; LGBTQ communities 13, 49–56, 58, 59, 61, 64–65, 72; non-belonging 27, 50–56, 59–66, 68, 73–74, 78, 83–85, 115; normative modes of 84, 116; QTPOC community 19, 54, 59, 62, 64, 67–69, 72, 74–75, 78, 83–84, 106, 116; racial melancholia 62, 68, 83–84, 115
black and brown (use as identifying term) 30
black feminist: theory 23, 25–28, 31–32, 42–44, 94–95, 103, 106, 108, 113–114, 118; activism 3, 9–12, 27–28, 31, 42–44, 94–95, 103, 106, 108, 114, 118; black queer feminist 19, 27, 31, 108, 113–114, 118; and feminism of colour 25–26, 28–29, 43–44, 103, 108, 118
Black Lesbian and Gay Centre, Peckham 4, 10, 29
Black Nationalism 9, 12, 13, 94
Black Power 7, 9, 12, 75
border thinking 23–24, 26, 43, 46, 114
Brighton 55, 58, 81, 97–98
Butler, Judith 5, 42, 64, 113

calling out 100, 104–105, 107
Caribbean feminisms 95, 118
categorical logic 41, 45, 46
class 8, 51, 60, 63, 66, 108, 118; middle-class 37, 67, 73, 79–80, 94; working-class 75, 89–90, 92–93, 116
coalition 7, 29–30, 46, 103
Cohen, C.J. 94, 96, 99, 117–118
coloniality 19, 22–23, 25–26, 30–31, 112–113, 116, 119; being 22, 26, 30, 36, 45, 47, 50, 70, 85–87, 89, 91, 109, 113–115, 119; colonisation 19, 32, 40, 64, 89, 94–95; heterosexualisation 95, 99; knowledge 22, 36, 50, 86, 91, 109, 119; modernity 26, 36, 70, 95; psychology 22–23, 33, 35–36; race, gender and sexuality 26, 45, 47, 50, 64, 85–87, 89, 92, 94–95, 97, 99, 116, 118; rationality 36; subjectivity 25, 113, 115–116; wounds 92, 94, 96, 117–118
collective 3–5, 7, 18, 27, 62, 79; possibilities of 22–23, 68, 83–84, 86, 110, 113–115, 118–119
community 15, 19, 40; creating/building community 69, 72, 76, 93, 96, 100, 106–109, 111, 115, 117; finding community 49–50, 59, 68, 72; lack of community 58; *see also* intersubjectivity; belonging
conflict 19, 78–80, 93, 100, 107–108, 118
corporeality 26, 37
Crenshaw, K. 44, 94, 112
critical consciousness 16, 18–19, 79, 87–88, 115; art 85–87; black (of African descent) 9, 42; conscientisation 27; critical decolonising consciousness 19, 50, 85–89, 91, 93, 96–97, 115; diasporic 6; Politically Black 4–5, 7
critical flippancy 78–80, 84
critical psychology 19–20, 22–23, 30–32, 112–113; Black feminist theory 42, 46–47; coloniality 47; embodiment and affect 35, 37, 40; feminist psychology 33, 37–40, 47; Foucauldian Discourse Analysis 34; Foucault 38; intersectionality 47; post-colonial 36, 38, 47; queer theory/psychology 37–39, 47; social constructionism 33–34, 40; subjectivity 33–37, 112; turn to language 33–35
cultural appropriation 77, 105

decoloniality 87, 113; anti-normativity 97; being 92, 95, 97, 117; critiques of modernity/rationality 36; critiques of universality 36; desire 92; erotic decolonial turn 94; love 22, 92–93, 96, 106, 110, 114, 117–119; potentialities 22, 96, 117; scholarship 27
decolonising 22, 84, 91–92, 106; decolonising queer politic 93, 96–99, 108, 116–119; gender and sexuality 3, 19, 22, 58, 81–82, 84–85, 87–91, 116; history 86
deficit approach 16, 18, 21
depressive position 83, 100, 115, 118
deviance 94; as resistance 96, 99, 117
dialogical encounter 24, 26–27, 31, 114
dialogue 91, 93, 96, 116–117
disability 11, 82, 83, 98
disciplinary decadence 23–24, 30, 113
disconnection 14, 50, 74–76
dis-identification 9, 23, 25, 58, 78, 80–81, 84, 98, 113, 116
dislocation 64–66, 68, 105
disorientation 19, 25–27, 46, 50, 54, 83; away from white heteronormativity 62, 67, 78, 98–99, 113–116; experience of racism 54, 79; of non-belonging 66, 68, 74–75; potential of 114; queerness of 51

embodiment 26, 28, 32–33, 69, 89; Chabani Manganyi 41; critical psychology 35, 37; embodied intersectionality 26, 30, 32, 46–47, 50, 53, 65, 74, 76–77, 80, 83, 89, 112, 114; embodied intersubjectivity 28, 40, 51, 61, 71, 73, 75–77, 83, 88, 112; embodied knowledge 83, 116; embodied recognition 75–76, 84, 115; queer embodiment 51–53, 62, 76, 80, 116
Eng, D.L. 25, 57, 62–67
epistemology 18, 27, 31, 34, 40; Haraway, D. 39; western 34, 36, 38
erotic, the 19, 22, 27, 31, 75–77, 83–84, 101, 110, 114, 116, 119; erotic autonomy 87, 94, 95; erotic decolonial turn 94; feeling-together-in-difference 110–111, 119
exclusion 16, 17, 54, 59, 61, 64, 65, 67, 105

faith 17, 51; Islam 51–53, 72; QTPOC groups 52–53; queerness 51–53, 72; secularism 51–52, 72
Fanon, Frantz 18, 23–26, 32, 36, 37, 40, 47, 50, 53–54, 92, 113–114; phenomenology 36, 41; psychoanalytic 40, 62
feeling 27, 31, 40, 71–72, 80, 112; feeling-one's-way 114
feeling-together-in-difference 19, 69, 71–73, 76, 83–84, 110–111, 115–116, 118–119; being a problem 83; depressive

position 83, 100, 110, 115, 118; emphatic projective identification 84, 115; erotics of 110–111, 119; feeling brown 83–84, 100, 110–111, 115, 118; feeling queerly raced 83–84, 96, 100, 110–111, 115, 118–119

harm 19, 22, 100, 109, 118
healing 76, 78–79
hermeneutics of suspicion 100, 105–106
heteronormativity 32; black 11–14, 81; brown 81; citizenship 95; European heterosexual inheritance 95, 99; heteropatriarchy 95, 99; homonormativity 2, 54, 67, 84, 115; racialised 92–93, 116; white/western 25, 50–51, 54, 62–64, 67, 78–80, 89, 92, 95, 99, 116
historical-racial schema 24–26, 113–114
HIV 11, 13, 21
homonationalism 2, 17, 49, 56–59, 74, 80, 97, 98
homophobia/biphobia/queerphobia/transphobia 14; addressing 96; african countries 89, 91; Asian communities 89, 91, 116; Asian countries 89, 91; Black communities 12–14, 17, 46, 49, 53, 56, 89–92, 94, 96, 116; church 12–13, 17, 53, 94; discrimination 11, 15; Muslim communities 58, 71; 'of colour' communities 18, 53; performance of 92–93, 96, 116; religious communities 53, 89; section 28, 11; violence 17–18

identity 15–16, 23, 29–30; ambivalences of 67; contextual/structural understandings of 16, 24, 33, 46; definition of people of colour 29–30, 102; definition of QTPOC 29–30, 101–103; fixed identity/culture 57–58, 102; fragmentation of 18–19, 21, 23, 43, 54–59, 70, 72–74, 80–81, 86–89, 97, 115–116, 119; intersectional identity 16, 18, 21–23, 46, 58, 73; LGBTQ 17; mixed race 102–103; political blackness 103; politics 103; white washing of identity 55–59, 63
immigration 7–9, 11, 17, 19, 62–64, 66; impossibility of return 64
interlocking *see* intersectionality
interpellation 5, 42, 66
intersectionality 10, 11, 13–14, 16, 19, 21, 23–26, 30, 43–47, 112–113; Black feminism and feminism of colour 43–47; class 90–92, 116; complexities of sexual and gender diversity in communities of colour 71–73, 85, 87–93, 116; disability 82–83; embodied intersectionality 26, 30, 32, 46–47, 50, 53, 65, 74, 76–77, 80, 83, 89, 112, 114; intersectional failure 44–45, 55; intersectional identity 16, 18, 21–23, 46, 58, 73; intersectional imagination 16; intersectional richness 18, 22, 55, 59, 62, 71, 74, 77, 97, 119; intersectional theoretical work 26, 43–47; intersection of race, gender, and sexuality 26, 30, 42–44, 46, 50, 55, 57–58, 60, 62, 64, 70–71, 73, 81–82, 85, 93, 99, 106, 112, 114–116, 118–119; intersection of racism, queerphobia and transphobia 15, 17–18, 46, 60, 64, 71, 73, 77, 81, 84, 92, 105–106, 112–115, 119; masculinity 87–93, 96, 116; power 46, 79–80, 92, 113; structural 30, 32, 42–44, 46–47, 60, 71, 73–74, 92; subjectivities 32, 42–43, 62, 70–71, 73, 113; trans 87–89, 116
intersubjectivity 25, 27, 30–31, 40, 57, 85, 92, 112–113; Embodied 28, 40, 51, 61, 71–74, 91; QTPOC 50, 61, 67–68, 71, 73–74, 77, 116
isolation 16, 54, 69, 74–75, 80
islamophobia 17, 51–52, 54, 61; LGBTQ communities 51–52, 58–59, 61

Johnson, K. 26–27, 38, 40, 112, 114
joy 22, 74, 76, 84, 101, 110, 116, 119
justice: community accountability 19, 96, 108–109, 118; punitive 107–109, 118; transformative 19, 93, 96, 100, 108–109, 111, 118–119

Lewis, G. 5, 9, 42, 94, 113
liberalism 5, 11, 38, 51–52, 57, 70, 91, 108; neoliberalism 97–98, 108–110
liberation 7, 8, 10–11, 13, 33, 75–76, 94, 103, 106, 114, 117–118
Lorde, A. 10, 23, 27, 42–43, 46, 50, 75–76, 96, 110
loss 62–67, 84–85, 115–116
love 76, 77, 92, 110; for community 92; *see also* decolonial; love
Lugones, M. 45–47, 93, 118

Maldonado-Torres, N. 28, 31, 45, 47, 87, 92, 94–95, 97, 113–114, 117
Mama, A. 5, 7, 9, 10, 23, 35, 42, 61, 112
Manganyi, C. 41
Mason-John, V. 11, 80–82, 98; and Khambatta, A. 8, 10–12, 74

mental distress and illness 14, 16–17, 62, 82
micro-affirmations 75
microaggressions 14, 17, 62, 67, 75, 78–79
minoritisation 17, 22–23, 64, 72–74, 77, 84, 106; internalisation of 58, 64, 73–74, 115
Minority Stress Model 14
Mirza, H. 7–9
multiplicity *see* intersectionality
Munoz, J.E. 9, 19, 25–26, 50, 67–69, 80, 83–84, 96, 100, 110, 112, 115, 118
Muslim 9, 17, 28, 51–53, 61, 71–72, 87; hijab 51–53; as homophobe 58, 61; sexuality 51–52; surveillance of 52–53, 72; white queer fantasies of 54, 72

nayak, S. 5, 19, 23–24, 26–27, 31–32, 42–43, 46–47, 59, 64–65, 106, 112–115
negation 50, 60, 64, 69, 83–84, 86, 103, 106, 108, 110, 115, 118
nepantlera 93, 117

objectification 22, 27, 30; black people and people of colour 53–54, 85, 92; psychological method 22, 27, 30, 114; self-objectification 92
objectivity 22, 27, 30, 33, 43, 114; Haraway, D. 39
ontology 18, 27, 31, 40, 45, 112; western 36, 38
orientalism 51–54
orientation: phenomenology 25, 50, 51; towards whiteness 59, 86; white heteronormativity 63, 67, 84, 89, 92, 94–95, 114

Pan-African 5–6, 12
paranoid reading 100, 104–107, 109–110, 118
pathologisation: black and brown communities 49, 50, 72, 92, 96, 99, 113; racialisation 54, 56, 72, 92, 99, 113, 116, 117
people of colour (definition/label) 29–30, 101–102
phenomenology 18, 24, 31, 33, 47, 114; Fanon, F. 36, 40, 41; interpretative phenomenological analysis 25; Manganyi, C. 41; 'queerly raced' phenomenology 18, 25–26, 28, 31, 113–114; queer phenomenology 25, 50, 67
Phoenix, A. 5, 13, 42, 46, 113
political blackness 4, 6–10, 27, 29, 35, 84, 99, 103
political organising in the UK 5, 6, 13, 27; Black (African/Caribbean descent) 5–6, 8, 27, 75, 99, 112; Black (politically Black and of African/Caribbean descent) lesbian, gay and bisexual 10–12, 21, 72, 74, 98–99, 112; Black (politically Black and of African/Caribbean descent) women/feminist 8–10, 99, 112; Black queer (African/Caribbean descent) 21, 99; Politically Black 7, 29, 99, 103, 112; Queer and Trans People of Colour 1, 4, 5, 18, 21, 27, 29, 67–68, 75–77, 81–83, 95, 99, 112, 115; South Asian 6–8, 112
post-colonial 6, 13, 32, 113; British context 3–5, 10, 19, 25–26, 58, 63, 70, 112, 114; gender and sexuality 19, 26
power: discourse and ideology 2, 5, 6, 8–9, 15, 18, 34–35, 37, 39, 40, 42–43, 46, 49, 51, 56–57, 59–61, 79–80, 85–86, 92–94, 96, 108–109, 116–118; intersectionality 46, 79–80, 92, 113; knowledge 22, 36, 39, 50, 86, 91, 109, 119; privilege 89–93; subject formation 23–24, 26, 31, 35, 40–43, 46–47, 49, 60, 63, 67, 112, 114
problematic behaviour 100, 106, 107
psychoanalysis 25, 40, 47, 62–63; Fanon, Frantz 36, 40–41, 62; feminist psychoanalysis 36; Manganyi, Chabani 41
psychology 22–23, 28, 30, 32; coloniality of 22–23, 33–37, 113; crisis in social psychology 33; critiques of 33–34, 37–39, 43, 47; maintenance/ reproduction of status quo 37, 39, 40, 113; traditional approaches to study of the individual/identity 33, 43
psychosocial 32, 40, 112
Puar, J.K. 2, 51–54, 57, 91, 98

QTPOC culture 76–77, 80–81, 101; QTPOC history 81–82, 85–86; shared language 78, 97
queer: expanding the definition of 96, 117; verb 103
queer and trans people of colour (definition/label) 29–30, 101
queerly raced: feeling queerly raced 22, 54, 83–84, 96, 100, 110–111, 115, 118–119; space 86
queer theory 26–28, 39–40, 80, 93, 96, 100, 105, 112, 114
Quijano, A. 19, 22, 26, 36, 113

racialisation–gendering–sexualisation 16, 19, 21, 25–26, 30, 41, 44–46, 51, 55, 57, 63, 93, 113–114; class 90–93, 116; difficulty of naming/speaking 60–62, 67, 70, 79; Europe's silent racialisations

60–62, 68, 70, 85, 87–89, 103, 113; making sense of 59–67, 70, 72, 78–79, 87–89, 103; masculinity 87–93, 96, 116; pathologisation 54, 93, 99, 113, 116, 117; queerness of 51, 53, 55; racialisation and heterosexualisation 95, 99, 116; racialised other as an illegitimate citizen 55–59; racialised other as a threat 55–57; racialised sexuality 93–96, 99; subjectivity 47, 62, 68, 85, 113, 116; trans 87–89, 116
racial melancholia 19, 22, 25, 57, 62–63, 65–68, 115; ego formation 67; haunting 60, 63–64, 67, 85, 115; impossibility of belonging 64, 83, 115; impossibility of return 64; loss of pre-colonial models of sexual and gender variance 64, 84–85, 115–116; possibilities of collective struggle 68–69, 83–84, 115, 118; subjectivity 67, 85
racism: colour-blindness 57, 61–62; commitment to racelessness 60, 62–63, 67–68, 70, 79, 85, 88, 103, 113, 115; denial of race/racism 55, 57–62, 70, 79, 85, 103; discrimination 6–10, 15, 44, 55–56; enlightenment 60, 63; harassment 15–16; historical erasure 86–87; internalised 58–59; law 7–9, 44, 56, 87, 94; LGBTQ communities 14–17, 51–55, 58; LGBTQ identity formation 17, 21, 51; minimising difference 58, 61–62; murder 7, 29, 87; pathologisation 49–50, 54, 56, 72, 92, 99, 113; policing 56, 87, 90–93; psychological defence against 92, 94; psychological impact 42, 54, 60; saying the unsayable 59–62, 68, 70, 79; silence 55, 57, 59–60, 85, 92; stereotypes 21, 55–58, 70, 92, 94, 116; structural 39, 49, 87–88; surveillance 52–56, 72, 90–92; traditional psychological approaches to understanding racism 38–39; violence 6–9, 27, 87, 116; whitewashing 19, 55–59, 63, 70, 97
reparative 19, 27, 40, 96, 100–101, 107, 109–110, 112, 114, 118–119
resilience 14–15, 17–18
respectability 17, 94–96, 117
rights: citizenship 17, 54, 56; human rights 51; LGBT rights and equalities in the UK 1–3, 11–12, 17; trans rights 2–3

safety 100, 106, 108–110; safe space 55–56, 104
Sedgwick, E. 26–27, 40, 100, 104–105, 107, 110, 112, 118

sexual and gender diversity/expression 50; black 94; black and brown expansiveness 84, 93, 116, 119; indigenous 95; QTPOC 51; as Western inventions 95
sexualities: Arabic 51–52; black 12, 16, 21, 94–96, 99; Muslim 51–52, 99; of colour 93, 99; repression 94; silence 93, 94; violence 94
Sivanandan, A. 7–8, 11, 27
skin of the social 24, 73–77
slavery 12, 38–39, 93–94
social support 13, 17–18, 22, 46, 58, 64, 70, 78–79, 81–82
solidarity 27–29, 75, 102–103; transnational/anti-imperial struggle 96–98; black cis/heterosexual and trans/queer 96, 117
spatiality 25, 54
stress 14–17, 50, 67
structural inequalities 19, 21, 33
subjectivity 5, 9, 12–13, 16, 19, 21, 23–26, 28, 30–31; always on the way 31, 43, 115, 119; becoming 7, 8, 10, 23–26, 28; black (African descent) British subjectivity 6–10, 13, 21; black (politically Black and of African/Caribbean descent) feminist 9–10, 42; British colonial subjectivity 6, 9, 13; class 90–92, 116; coloniality 25, 40–41, 46, 53, 68, 87, 89, 94, 109, 113; contextual/structural understandings of 16–17, 24–26, 33, 40, 42–43, 46–47, 49, 60–61, 73–74, 90, 112–114, 119; critical psychology 33–34, 37; fragmentation of 18, 19, 21, 23, 43, 54–59, 70, 72–74, 80–81, 86–89, 114, 116, 119; internal world/external world 66; intersectional 32, 42–43, 47, 70; intersubjectivity 25, 27, 30–31, 40, 57, 68, 73, 85, 112; masculinity 87–93, 96, 116; negotiation and understanding of 46, 54, 58–66, 70, 72–73, 89, 112; neo-colonial 95; new forms of subjectivity 64, 81, 84, 116, 119; 'of colour' 8, 21, 57; politically black 7–10, 13, 35; power 35, 41–43, 46, 60, 90, 93; psychical erasure of 63, 65, 87, 89; QTPOC 19, 21, 23, 35, 46, 53–54, 57, 59, 60–61, 65–66, 68, 70, 73, 81, 85–87, 112, 114; queer Muslim 52–54; racial melancholia 66–67, 84–85; subject formation 23–24, 26, 31, 35, 40–43, 46–47, 49, 60, 63, 67, 112, 114; trans people of colour 87–89, 116; violence 46, 100, 116
survival 9, 79–80, 82–83, 86, 94, 106

temporality 24–25
third person consciousness 25–26, 45, 54, 59
trauma 14, 16, 19, 46, 64, 96, 100, 105–107, 111, 118; impact on health 82; non-belonging 50, 61

universality 24, 28, 31, 33, 40, 43–44, 52, 62, 72, 113, 119

validation 78–79
violence 100, 107–108; anti-colonial counter violence 100, 106; anti-violence movements 108; colonial 100, 105–106; state 108, 116
visibility 74, 76, 82
visual methods 28

wellbeing 14, 17, 82–83, 108
Western LGBTQ movements/communities: Britishness 58, 59; coming out in majority white LGBTQ communities 58–59, 61, 64; globalisation of 95, 97, 99; imperialism 52; islamophobia 52–54, 57–59, 61; racism 14–17, 51, 52–59, 68, 71; right wing 57; secularism 52; sexual and gender diversity constructed in whiteness 64, 72, 74, 81, 87–88, 97, 115–116; queer citizenship 54, 57–59; white hegemony 64, 70; whiteness 15–17, 22, 54–55, 57, 59, 64; *see also* whiteness
whiteness 15, 19, 54, 78, 80; ambivalence towards 66–67; attaining/losing whiteness 63–64, 66; being 63; LGBTQ narratives/communities 15–17, 22, 54–55, 57, 59, 64, 71–72; manichean dynamic between Black and White 41; resistance to 75, 79–80, 82; white gaze 25, 40, 49–55, 72, 92–94; white hegemony 19, 61, 63–64, 66, 69–70; white heteronormativity 25, 50–51, 54, 62–64, 67, 78–80, 89, 92, 95, 99, 116; white normativity 16, 22, 54–55, 72, 74, 80, 84, 87, 89, 99, 116; white supremacy 14, 16–17, 19, 32–33, 38, 43, 47, 86, 89, 91–93, 102, 115–116; whitewashing 19, 55–59, 63, 70, 97
Windrush 5

zone of non-being 36, 63